Virginia Woolf was born in London in 1882 and died in 1941. She and her husband, Leonard Woolf, were leaders of the famous 'Bloomsbury Group'.

Her first books were novels, and at the time of her death she had won a foremost place in English fiction, but she also ranks high among literary critics and essayists.

Joan Russell Noble was born in Sussex and educated at the Convent of the Sacred Heart and at the Brighton and Hove High School. She read English Literature at King's College, University of London. She has worked in London on magazine groups as feature writer and fiction editor. *Recollections of Virginia Woolf* is her first publication. She is married to journalist Peter Browne – great grandson of Phiz (Hablôt Knight Browne), Dickens's illustrator. They have two sons and live in Twickenham.

Michael Holroyd, who was born in London in 1935, studied science at Eton and read literature in Maidenhead Public Library. He is the author of *Hugh Kingsmill: A Critical Biography* (1964), *A Dog's Life*, a novel (1969), *The Best of Hugh Kingsmill*, *Lytton Strachey: A Biography*, *Lytton Strachey and the Bloomsbury Group*, *Unreceived Opinions* and *Augustus John*. Michael Holroyd is currently working on his biography of George Bernard Shaw.

RECOLLECTIONS
OF VIRGINIA WOOLF

Edited by
Joan Russell Noble
with an introduction by
Michael Holroyd

SPHERE BOOKS LTD

Published by the Penguin Group
27 Wrights Lane, London w8 5tz, England
Viking Penguin Inc., 40 West 23rd Street, New York, New York 10010, USA
Penguin Books Australia Ltd, Ringwood, Victoria, Australia
Penguin Books Canada Ltd, 2801 John Street, Markham, Ontario, Canada L3R 1B4
Penguin Books (NZ) Ltd, 182–190 Wairau Road, Auckland 10, New Zealand

Penguin Books Ltd, Registered Offices: Harmondsworth, Middlesex, England

First published in Great Britain by Peter Owen 1972
Published in Penguin Books 1975
Published in Cardinal by Sphere Books 1989
1 3 5 7 9 10 8 6 4 2

This collection copyright © Joan Russell Noble 1972
Introduction copyright © Michael Holroyd 1973
All rights reserved

Printed and bound in Great Britain by
Richard Clay Ltd, Bungay, Suffolk

For PETER

and for Barnaby and Christopher

... men come with their violins; wait; count; nod; down come their bows. And there is ripple and laughter like the dance of olive trees ...

'Like' and 'like' and 'like' – but what is the thing that lies beneath the semblance of the thing? Now that lightning has gashed the tree and the flowering branch has fallen ... let me see the thing. There is a square; there is an oblong. The players take the square and place it upon the oblong. They place it very accurately; they make a perfect dwelling-place.

Rhoda – *The Waves*

Contents

CONTENTS

List of Illustrations

The author and publisher are grateful to the copyright owners for permission to reproduce the pictures.

I should also like to...

Acknowledgements

I AM grateful to the following for kindly granting me permission to quote from copyright sources: the Author's Literary Estate and the Hogarth Press for *The Waves* by Virginia Woolf; Professor Quentin Bell and Chatto & Windus Ltd for *Old Friends* by Clive Bell; the Cambridge University Press (copyright 1942) and the Society of Authors for E. M. Forster's Rede Lecture (abridged version); Mr David Garnett, Chatto & Windus Ltd and Harcourt, Brace Jovanovich, Inc. for *The Flowers of the Forest*; Mr Duncan Grant for an article previously published; Mr Christopher Isherwood for *Virginia Woolf*, written at the time of her death, and for an introduction, Curtis Brown Ltd and Simon & Schuster, Inc. (copyright 1966); the Author's Literary Estate and Atlantic-Little, Brown & Company (*In My Own Time*, copyright 1955, 1960, 1966, 1969) for letters from Virginia Woolf to Mr John Lehmann which are mentioned in his article; and the Author's Literary Estate for various references to letters from Virginia Woolf.

I am particularly indebted to Miss Rosamond Lehmann for her adaptation of *For Virginia Woolf* (*Penguin New Writing* 7, 1941, edited by John Lehmann).

I should also like to express my thanks to Mrs Valerie Eliot, widow and Literary Executor of T. S. Eliot, for an article written by him in 1941; A. D. Peters & Co. for *Virginia Woolf* by the late Dame Rose Macaulay; and to Mr Nigel Nicolson, Executor for his mother, the Hon. Vita Sackville-

West, for permission to include recollections written by her in the form of a letter to a friend.

The latter three articles, Mr Duncan Grant's, and Mr William Plomer's second contribution to the book were first published in *Horizon* magazine, shortly after Virginia Woolf's death in 1941. They were commissioned by Mr Cyril Connolly, founder and editor of the magazine.

I am particularly grateful to the producer, Stephen Peet, to Malcolm Muggeridge, and to the BBC, for permission to include in this new edition the full transcript of the BBC-Television conversations which took place between Leonard Woolf and Malcolm Muggeridge at Monks House, Rodmell, in March 1967.

JRN 1975

Introduction

THE third child of Leslie Stephen by his second marriage, Virginia Woolf came to believe that the rival streams of her mother's and father's traditions 'dashed together and flowed confused but not harmonized in her blood'. From her mother she inherited her sensitivity and artistic taste; from her father intellectual power and a neurotic conscience. She was educated at home and the influence of her father was especially strong.

Leslie Stephen's career was an epitome of Victorian intellectualism. Brought up in the faith of the established church, he had gone up to Cambridge and entered Holy Orders. Then, turning to agnosticism, he left for London and a career in literature. Founder of the *Dictionary of National Biography* and author of critical and philosophical works, he had grown celebrated as a skilled expositor of the agnosticism that permeated Victorian thought after Darwin's *Origin of Species*. Less tough than Thomas Huxley, less bleak than Herbert Spencer, he shared with many of the brilliant scholars who were his friends a core of poetry encased within the hard shell of pedantry.

For these dons, judges and headmasters, earnest rationalists all of them, who moved so magisterially within their cathedral closes, quadrangles of ancient colleges or the secluded squares of Kensington, nursed, beneath their assured exteriors, fears about the stability of this world as well as the existence of the next. Increasingly they found their happiness at the circumference of their lives, at remote places where the railways could now conveniently carry them – the coast of Cornwall or the mountains of Switzerland, where they might again sense the mystery of life that had so logically been explained away behind their desks at home.

Leslie Stephen was already in his fiftieth year when, as the result of a contraceptive failure, Virginia was born. The days of his athletic feats on the river or struggling up big peaks between Swiss guides were over, though relics of these exploits – the dusty cup on the mantelpiece, the rusted alpenstocks that leant against the bookcase – encumbered their gloomy house at Hyde Park Gate. Yet he was still capable, while on holiday, of going on a 'potter' of thirty miles or so. In the summer the family often went to Talland House at St Ives 'at the very toenail of England', and here Virginia was at her happiest. These childhood summers left sea-memories that haunt her novels – especially *Jacob's Room, To the Lighthouse* and *The Waves* – in their images, rhythms and colours, the blues and greens, that shine through her work and give it a translucent glow.

London, by contrast, was overcast. If the sea symbolized the poetry of life, Hyde Park Gate came to represent the threat of death, madness and disaster. Virginia's upbringing, though outwardly secure, was interspersed by a series of traumatic shocks. From an early age her half-sister Laura had shown disconcerting symptoms of mental instability; then her cousin J. K. Stephen, following an accident, also began to go mad, violently pursuing Virginia's half-sister Stella Duckworth. Since 1888, when he suddenly collapsed, Leslie Stephen's health had not been good. He was looked after devotedly by Julia, his wife, until, worn and harassed, she suddenly died in 1895. 'Her death,' declared Virginia, 'was the greatest disaster that could happen.'

The period between her mother's death and that of her father nine years later was filled with darkness. The lease of Talland House was sold and Virginia suffered the first of a series of nervous breakdowns that were so dreadfully to punctuate her life. When in 1897, within a year of her marriage, Stella Duckworth died, the old man came increasingly to rely on his two daughters Vanessa and Virginia. Lovable to his friends, he was ruthless with his family, inflicting on them a savage emotional blackmail. The Stephens were devoted to catastrophe. Like all their tragedies, his illness was accompanied by a chorus of female lamentations that magnified and funereally enriched his last agonizing months.

For Virginia this time was made more horrible by the improper advances of her half-brother, George Duckworth. 'I still shiver with shame,' she wrote many years afterwards, 'at the memory of my half-brother, standing me on a ledge, aged about six or so, exploring my private parts.' Now, while her father lay dying of cancer three or four floors below, George would fling himself upon Virginia's bed, kissing and embracing her in order, so he later explained, to administer comfort. The result was, Quentin Bell writes, that 'in sexual matters she was from this time terrified back into a posture of frozen and defensive panic'. She felt her life had been spoilt before it had begun.

Her father's death in 1904 was followed by another of Virginia's breakdowns: the birds sang piercingly in Greek while King Edward VII, among the azaleas, swore in the foulest language. The absurdity reached a pitch of nightmare, and she attempted to commit suicide by throwing herself out of a window. But Leslie Stephen's death – as with a similar situation in *The Years* – had given his children freedom. By moving into Bloomsbury they escaped the galling interference of their relations and started a new life by meeting their brother Thoby's Cambridge friends – Clive Bell, Lytton Strachey, Leonard Woolf and others who form the nucleus of the Bloomsbury Group.

The chronicle of disaster, however, was not yet at an end. Following a visit to Greece, Thoby died of typhoid. One partial result of this was that Vanessa Stephen agreed to marry Clive Bell. Virginia was half pleased, half distressed; but when Vanessa had a child, she was undisguisably jealous and to injure her sister embarked on a prolonged and pointless flirtation with Clive Bell.

Men as lovers played no part in Virginia's imagination. It was with women she tended to fall in love – with Madge Vaughan, Violet Dickinson and even her sister Vanessa. The love she felt for them was akin to that of a daughter for her mother. When Hilton Young proposed marriage, it was no more than a game to her: nothing real. But when Lytton Strachey proposed, she briefly accepted because, since he was homosexual, she might enjoy with him an affectionate brother-and-sister marriage unthreatened by the horror of sex.

She wanted to be married. To remain a spinster would, in the eyes of the world, be 'failure', and she was acutely aware of this. The Strachey experiment came to nothing, but in 1912, after some hesitation, she accepted a proposal from Leonard Woolf. 'The obvious advantages of marriage stand in my way . . . I feel no physical attraction to you,' she assured him. '. . . And yet your caring for me as you do almost overwhelms me. It is so real, and so strange.'

Two months later, on 10 August 1912, they were married at St Pancras Registry Office, after an engagement which, in the words of her sister Vanessa, was 'an exhausting and bewildering thing even to the bystanders'. In Virginia's own mind, so Quentin Bell tells us at the beginning of the second volume of his biography,* this 'seemed a very good way of getting married' to the strange wild man, her husband. During the ceremony a thunderstorm broke out and the half-blind Registrar, temporarily deprived of most of his faculties, began muddling the names – at which Vanessa interceded to ask how she should go about changing the name of Quentin, her younger son. Despite this confusion, Virginia and Leonard at length emerged officially married into the rain.

Iceland was where they had planned to enjoy their honeymoon: but eventually they set off in the more orthodox direction of the Mediterranean. It was a trying time. The heat was bad; the food was not good; and Virginia, who was reading Charlotte M. Yonge, found it impossible to respond physically to Leonard. Although she cheerfully continued expecting to have children, she also confessed to Ka Cox that 'I might still be Miss S.' There seemed some unfathomable inhibition that made male lust, even when compounded with love, if not horrific, quite incomprehensible to her. The physical act of intercourse was not even funny: it was cold. Leonard, who must have hoped to thaw her sexual frigidity, regretfully accepted the facts and soon brought the word in line with the deed by persuading her that they should have

* *Virginia Woolf. A Biography. Volume Two, Mrs Woolf, 1912–41.*

no children. It was a sensible decision for, though she could never contemplate her sister's fruitfulness without envy, children with their wetness and noise would surely have killed off the novels in her: and it was about novel-writing that she cared most.

After five years of marriage, so Quentin Bell indiscreetly reveals, Leonard, 'whose passionate nature was never in doubt', took a mistress. Her name was the Hogarth Press and, despite some odd deviationist experiments in the Bloomsbury manner, he would consent to share her with no man. For Virginia the Press was, at least for a time, therapeutic: she could escape from being a novelist and become a compositor and packer. She needed to escape. From the end of 1912 onwards she had suffered from acute anxiety, from depression, gnawing headaches and nights of sleeplessness in which the sense of her own futility, like a weed, rose to terrible proportions. The tortured intensity with which she had written her first novel, *The Voyage Out*, followed by a disillusioning douche of cold proofs, was breaking her up. Within herself she carried a more-than-ordinary tiredness, impossible to reach. In September 1913, overcome with guilt and misery, she attempted to kill herself – and nearly succeeded.

Her recovery was slow; agonizingly slow and intermittent. She was afflicted with states of garrulous mania, with comas, bouts of monstrous physical self-aversion, and a virulent animosity towards Leonard. 'She won't see Leonard at all,' Jean Thomas recorded, 'and has taken against all men. She says the most malicious and cutting things she can think of to everyone and they are so clever that they always hurt.'

The gradual improvement in her health was assisted by the good notices her novel received, which acted as certificates of her sanity. Even so, it was not until the autumn of 1915 that she could begin once more to follow a normal life. These two lost years, spent largely in the land of her own delusions, overshadowed the rest of her career and affected the pattern of her marriage. Leonard, who had come under very considerable strain, took to politics and gardening as part-time escapes into less intense areas of reality. Since she might easily relapse into madness, and each attack threatened to be more difficult to recover from, he had to watch her vigilantly and get to know her illness with the real intimacy of enemies. Praise and encouragement were oxygen and hydrogen to Virginia, and he supplied them in measured quantities continually, blowing away the irrational pain, the sense of failure that threatened to lay waste her life. To outsiders he was cast as the family dragon – a part that in some ways suited his temperament well. He had to make sure that Virginia led as vegetative an existence as possible, supported by good food, cushioned with plenty of rest. She must avoid too many visitors and anything that might tire her physically or mentally. Yet she was a born writer. Living, breathing, meant writing to her, with all the awful agitations and agonies so incomprehensible to non-writers. 'Nothing is real unless I write it,' she once admitted. And so Leonard trained himself to spot the smallest symptom of an oncoming attack, and take quick action to avoid it. Over the years, while she gave birth to a unique series of novels, essays, short stories, he acted as their midwife, making sure after each book was born that she could come back and face the ordeal of writing another.

Yet the threat of madness was always present. 'I feel certain I am going mad again,' she wrote to him on the morning of Friday, 28 March 1941. 'I feel we can't go through another of those terrible times. And I shan't recover this time. I begin to hear voices, and I can't concentrate. So I am doing what seems the best thing to do . . .' She made her way across the water meadows to the river, forced a large stone into her pocket, and drowned herself. Her last sentence, reminiscent of Hazlitt's dying words, is a tribute to her own indomitable courage and the unwavering devotion of Leonard: 'I don't think two people could have been happier than we have been.'

MICHAEL HOLROYD

Ann Stephen
(Mrs Richard Synge)

As a small child I spent most of my time among the servants and did not know many of the grown-up members of my parents' circle. Virginia, in particular, was little more than a name with a shadowy and rather mysterious figure attached to it. There is, though, one encounter with her which I remember very clearly. It must have taken place in the early twenties when I was about six. I was, as usual, playing in the gardens in Gordon Square when she walked in through the main entrance. She was with someone else and when they came near to where I was playing she spoke to me and I spoke to her; it was nothing special, just a short exchange between aunt and niece, but it impressed me because of what I had heard while having my elevenses in the kitchen. The servants of Bloomsbury were a community of their own and gossip passed from one house to another largely on the lips of charwomen. That day the talk had been about Mrs W and, although I could not make out all that was being said, I certainly knew who Mrs W was. The general tone of the conversation was set by the remark, 'Well! We all know that genius is next door to madness, don't we?' and this had conjured up a picture in my mind of a wild and distraught person, perhaps eccentrically dressed, perhaps striding about and spouting poetry while quite unaware of all that was going on around her, perhaps tearing her hair, yelling or making some other sort of scene. But that wasn't at all the Mrs W I met. This one was quietly dressed in dark clothes , wearing a hat, and talking to a companion as she strolled round the gardens. What is more, she noticed me and spoke to me in a far more friendly and interested way than most of the grown-ups I met. She was much less like my picture of a mad genius than those intimidating Stracheys who were also to be seen in the square.

Another memory which stands out in my mind dates from about 1930. Virginia and Leonard invited me to dine and go to the theatre with them. It was a very grand occasion for me and I was a little afraid that I might be out of my depth in such august company, but again I was pleasantly surprised. Of course the wine may have had something to do with it, but I remember feeling unusually self-assured. I enjoyed their conversation and it appeared to me that they enjoyed mine. It all seemed very grown-up – that is, until the dessert. This was fresh pineapple which was a favourite with me. I ate an enormous amount, got very sticky and was dubbed a Pine Pig, and I was referred to as such for some time afterwards. We went to the theatre by taxi, which also seemed tremendously grand to me. On the way Virginia described what it would be like at the theatre. As she talked – and I questioned – the description got more and more extravagant: the King and Queen would be here, they would be wearing their crowns sparkling with diamonds and rubies, their embroidered silk robes and ermine cloaks; as they entered the Royal Box the whole audience would rise to its feet and cheer and sing while the orchestra played 'God Save the King'. Of course I didn't believe a word of it but it was a splendid game and, besides, I was a bit above myself with the wine and the pineapple and the company. We had barely taken our seats, though, when the King and Queen *did* come into the Royal Box, and the audience *did* rise and sing while the orchestra played 'God Save the King'. True, they were not so gorgeously dressed as we had pretended, but Queen Mary was wearing a lot of jewellery and was an impressive figure. Moreover, the Duke and Duchess of York were there too, so there was no sense of disappointment. The play we saw was *The Calendar*, by Edgar Wallace, but the Royal Family made more impression on us than the actors and, on the way home in the taxi, we speculated about how they lived. Virginia said that she did not know they would be there, but I have often thought that perhaps she did.

Later, when I was away at boarding school and Sunday afternoon was supposed to be spent writing letters, I remembered that evening and decided to send Virginia a similarly embroidered account of school life. Virginia replied in kind and we carried on a nonsense correspondence for several months. She also gave me copies of some of her books. I do not remember much of the contents of the letters and, unfortunately, they and the books vanished during the war. On the other hand, I do remember very clearly the great pleasure in writing to Virginia and in getting letters from her.

The last coherent memory I have of Virginia is at a gathering in my room in Newnham when I was an undergraduate. Obviously, my friends who were reading English wanted to meet her, and they pestered me to arrange a meeting at which she would expound her ideas about The Novel but equally obvious was the fact that this was not Virginia's style. After consulting her it was arranged that she should come and dine with me and one or two of my friends in my room, and that after dinner a few more people who wanted to meet her were to be invited in for coffee and round-the-fire conversation. The evening went well. It was not that anything new or startling was said. Virginia, of course, told us how lucky we were to go to the university and have a proper education; we, or some of us, said how much luckier she was to have had the run of a good library and the company of the literary world without being burdened with listening to lectures or writing essays. The matter of the discussion was predictable, but Virginia's lack of pretentiousness and her natural interest in what we young women were thinking and doing brought out the best in all of us. Even those guests who, beforehand, had seemed to me a bit mouselike and dull found their tongues and had something interesting to say.

Duncan Grant

I FIRST knew Virginia Stephen when she and her brother Adrian took No. 29 Fitzroy Square, soon after her sister Vanessa married Clive Bell. It was a house on the south-west corner of the square with a view of the two fine Adam façades. It was a derelict square. The houses of the great had gradually decayed and were taken as offices, lodgings, nursing homes and small artisans' workshops.

I had taken for a studio two rooms on the second floor of a house on the same side of the square. There was certainly not much gentility left in the district; the only relic of grandeur was a beadle to march round the square and keep order among the children, in a top hat and a tailcoat piped with red and brass buttons. The Stephens were the only people I remember who had a complete house there; complete with their cook Sophie Farrell, their maid Maud, a front-door bell and a dog, Hans. A close friendship sprang up between Adrian Stephen and myself, and I had only to tap at the window of the ground-floor room to be let in. 'That Mr Grant gets in everywhere,' Maud once remarked to Virginia. But irregular as my visits were, in a sense they soon became frequent enough to escape notice.

The house was conveniently divided to suit the inhabitants. On the ground floor was Adrian's study lined with books. Behind was the dining-room. The first floor was entirely a drawing-room – the room least used in the house. It was a pleasantly proportioned room, with long windows overlooking the square. It had a green carpet, red brocade curtains; a Dutch 'Portrait of a Lady' and Watts's portrait of Sir Leslie Stephen were the only pictures on the walls. In the back part of the room there was an instrument called a pianola, into which one put rolls of paper punctured by small holes. You bellowed with your feet and Beethoven or Wagner would appear.

Anyone coming into the room might have thought that Adrian was a Paderewski – the effort on the bellows gave him a swaying movement very like that of a great performer, and his hands were hidden.

I do not remember that Virginia ever performed on this instrument, but it must have played a part in her life, for Adrian on coming home from work would play in the empty room by the hour. Entirely empty it nearly always was and kept spotlessly clean.

It was here that Virginia sometimes saw her less intimate friends and it was here that the dog Hans made a mess on the hearthrug when Lady Strachey was paying her first visit, and no mention was made of the fact by either lady.

The more lively rooms were Virginia's own workroom above this, and Adrian's downstairs. Her room was full of books untidily arranged and a high table at which she would write standing. The windows on this floor were double. She was very sensitive to sound, and the noise from the mews and street was severe. The time she gave to her writing was two and a half hours in the morning. She never, I believe, wrote for more than this time, but very regularly.

The study on the ground floor had the air of being

much lived in. It was to this room that their friends came on Thursday evenings – a continuation of those evenings which began in Gordon Square before Thoby Stephen died and before Vanessa married. It was there that what has since been called 'Bloomsbury' for good or ill came into being.

About 10 o'clock in the evening people used to appear and continue to come at intervals till 12 o'clock at night, and it was seldom that the last guest left before two or three in the morning. Whisky, buns and cocoa were the diet and people talked to each other. If someone had lit a pipe he would sometimes hold out the lighted match to Hans the dog, who would snap at it and put it out. Conversation; that was all. Yet many people made a habit of coming, and few who did so will forget those evenings.

Among those who constantly came in early days were Charles Sanger, Theodore Llewelyn Davies, Desmond MacCarthy, Charles Tennyson, Hilton Young, Lytton Strachey.

It was certainly not a 'salon'. Virginia Stephen in those days was not at all the sort of hostess required for such a thing. She appeared very shy and probably was so, and never addressed the company. She would listen to general arguments and occasionally speak, but her conversation was mainly directed to someone next to her. Her brother's Cambridge friends she knew well by this time, but I think there was always something a little aloof and even a little fierce in her manner to most men at the time I am speaking of. To her women friends, especially older women like Miss Pater and Miss Janet Case, who had taught her Greek, she was more open and less re-served. They were alive to her, by remembrance as well as presence, and had already their place in her imagi-nation as belonging to the world she knew and had left –

that life with her parents and her half-brothers at Hyde Park Gate. Henceforward she and her brother and sister had tacitly agreed to face life on their own terms.

I do not think that her new existence had 'become alive' to Virginia's imagination in those first years. She gave the impression of being so intensely receptive to any experience new to her, and so intensely interested in facts that she had not come across before, that time was necessary to give it a meaning as a whole. It took the years to complete her vision of it.

It is very difficult for one who is no writer to attempt to describe so subtle a thing as the 'feeling' of long ago. But I must make the attempt to explain why it was that the effect of these young people on a contemporary was so remarkable. To begin with they were not Bohemians. The people I had come across before who had cut themselves off from respectable existence had been mainly painters and Bohemians. If the Stephens defied the conventions of their particular class, it was from being intellectually honest. They had suffered much, had struggled and finally arrived at an attitude of mind which I think had a great influence on their friends. If it was an influence Virginia Stephen and her sister were unconscious of the fact.

The impression generally given must have been that these two young women were absorbing the ideas of their new Cambridge friends. And of course this was true up to a point. Saxon Sydney-Turner, Clive Bell, Lytton Strachey, Maynard Keynes were willing to discuss anything and everything with them or before them. It was a gain all round. What the Cambridge of that time needed was a little feminine society. It was a little arid, and if it took almost everything seriously it had mostly left the Arts out of account. It took some things religiously. 'This is my Bible' was said by one, pointing to the *Principia Ethica*, by G. E. Moore. This eminent philosopher was certainly the overwhelming influence on these young men. Interpretations of the 'good' and the value of certain states of mind were a frequent subject of discussion; and these apostolic young men found to their amazement that they could be shocked by the boldness and scepticism of two young women.

To be intimate with Virginia Stephen in those days was not to be on easy terms. Indeed the greater the intimacy, the greater the danger – the danger of sudden outbursts of scathing criticism. I have the impression that no one had much encouragement for anything they produced. Nor was it looked for. Nothing was expected save complete frankness (of criticism) and a mutual respect for the point of view of each. To work for immediate success never entered anyone's head, perhaps partly because it seemed out of the question. Virginia Stephen was working on her first novel, *The Voyage Out*. It took seven years to finish. But I do not remember that this was thought to be an out-of-the-way length of time in which to produce a novel.

The inner fierceness of her attitude to which I have already alluded is worth remembering, and will possibly surprise those who only knew her in later life when it seemed to have entirely disappeared or to have found expression in quite other ways.

It then expressed itself sometimes, as I have said, by an appearance of acute shyness. Upon an unforeseen introduction, for instance, there was an expression of blazing defiance, a few carefully chosen banalities, and a feeling of awkwardness. It came from a sort of variant of Cézanne's '*grapin dessous*', which made her literally turn tail from misadventure. As when she saw Mrs Humphry

Ward advancing along a narrow passage in the Louvre and hid herself behind a totally inadequate post.

No one so beautiful and so fierce could give offence except to the very stupid. But she was capable of inspiring feelings of respect in the most philistine.

This shyness or fierceness was a necessary self-defence in her war with the world. The world must, she surmised, accept her on her own terms or not at all.

If these notes have any interest it is because they may to some revive the memory, to others suggest the existence, of that seemingly very different Virginia Woolf known to a variety of people in later years. Marriage and possibly a growing appreciation of her work had the effect of seeming to make her very much more at ease in the world.

John Lehmann

(A lecture delivered at
various times and in
various places in the USA)

IN the autumn of 1930 Leonard and Virginia Woolf were looking for a new young manager for the Hogarth Press, the publishing business they had founded and built up themselves.

By that time the Press, though comparatively small and run on the simplest lines, had become a successful and well-known publishing centre. It had four extremely valuable advantages. It had always published Virginia Woolf's works since the First World War, but after the success of *Orlando* in 1928 Virginia was no longer a highly thought of experimental novelist of limited appeal, but a best-seller. Her friend Vita Sackville-West – Mrs Harold Nicolson – had had several books of travel published by the Press, but in 1930 she had produced a novel called *The Edwardians*, which had one of the greatest successes in the history of the Press. The third advantage it had was the International Psycho-Analytical Library, which included the works of Sigmund Freud. At the suggestion of Lytton Strachey's brother James, a keen student of psychoanalysis, Leonard, with great shrewdness, and against the advice of some distinguished old hands in the publishing world, had taken on the English-speaking rights of the Library in the early twenties. It flourished exceedingly. The fourth advantage was, of course, Leonard and Virginia's own names as leaders of what was known as the Bloomsbury Group. Among intellectuals it was a much coveted prize to be accepted for publication by the Hogarth Press. It had begun its work in the tiniest way possible in 1917, and by the end of 1919 had published only five books; but one of them was T. S. Eliot's *Poems*, another was Virginia's own first experimental attempt, *Kew Gardens*, and a third was Katherine Mansfield's *Prelude*. Two of them had been printed and bound by Leonard and Virginia themselves.

It was a much coveted prize; but not necessarily at the time a financially rewarding one. All his life Leonard tended to despise the orthodox tenets of publishing about professional organization and distribution. There is no doubt, however, in my mind, that the shoe-string on which the Press was run did tend to reduce its penetration of the bookshops, though it could not hold back an author like Virginia Woolf once she had become a best-seller.

The Hogarth Press was named after Hogarth House in Richmond where they were living when they began printing and publishing. In 1924 they moved to No. 52 Tavistock Square in Bloomsbury. Leonard and Virginia lived upstairs, and the activities of the Press were concentrated in the basement – a rather ramshackle basement, as was the case in many of the old Bloomsbury houses. The front room, looking on to the square, was the general office, in which there were as a rule not more than two or three girls at work, whose business it was to deal with the orders, make out the invoices, pack up the books and handle the general correspondence. Leading out of that basement front room was a longish, dark corridor, piled with binders' packets of recently published books. On one side was the former scullery, in which Leonard had installed the treadle printing press, still used for occasional small and special books. At the end of the corridor was a humble room, which had probably been a kind of pantry in earlier days. In this room the manager was installed. His duties were not only the general supervision of relations with printers, binders and booksellers, but also the handling of publicity and the interviewing of would-be authors as well as salesmen; and, twice a year, acting as traveller all over the country for the season's new books. Quite a big and responsible job, in fact, for a young man to tackle, who had little or no professional experience. He worked, of course, under Leonard's direction and advice; but as Leonard, in spite of his charm, sense of humour and outstanding qualities of mind and sensibility, could be a very exacting task-master, nervy and obstinate in petty argument, it is not really surprising that there were frequent changes in the post of manager.

Outside this manager's cell, visible from its gloomy window that was always stuck, was a small passage open to the sky, which connected the corridor with the studio at the back. I am going to anticipate now, and quote from an article on Virginia Woolf which I wrote for a French literary review just before the end of the Second World War. This is the opening paragraph:

When I think of Virginia Woolf, the picture that first springs to my mind is of her workroom in Tavistock Square. It was a big, square studio with a skylight, built on to the basement. It was used by the Hogarth Press as a stock-room, and there in the midst of an ever-encroaching forest of books was her desk, stuffed and littered with papers, letters and innumerable half-finished manuscripts. I was learning my job as Manager then, in the little back room, and she would pass my window every day as she went into her work. She would stay there for hours, writing steadily; if it wasn't a novel, it was an article, or a short story, or her own diary; I don't think she was happy unless her pen was moving over the paper in that thin, elegant, intellectual handwriting with the beautiful flourishes; and that is the reason why, after her death, so many unknown treasures were found among her papers, though only too few were in a finished state. Sometimes she would move over to the disused scullery that had been converted by Leonard Woolf into a printing-room, and help set up type for the occasional small volumes that were still produced entirely by the Hogarth Press; and sometimes, when a new book had just been published and there was a heavy rush of orders to be dealt with, she would come into the front room and work with the staff, tying up parcels and and sticking on labels. The young poets and novelists who came to leave manuscripts, hoping desperately that the so famous, elusive author would read and approve their works, never guessed that she was there in person, working unobtrusively under their very eyes.

To return to the sequence of my story. As I have said, in the autumn of 1930 Leonard and Virginia were once more looking for a manager. It so happened that I, who had gone down from Cambridge in the early summer, had just completed work on a first book of poems. At Cambridge, two of my closest friends had been Julian Bell and the young don, George Rylands, known as Dadie. Julian was a poet, with whom for years I had endless happy discussion and arguments about poetry. He was also the son of Clive and Vanessa Bell, and therefore Virginia's nephew. Through him, the Woolfs knew quite a lot about me already. As for George Rylands, I was never under his tutorship, but he knew my sister Rosamond well, and from the first he took a friendly and perceptive interest in my poetry, coaxing and teasing me out of my lushest romantic impulses. He had been published by the Hogarth Press, and he had also been the first of the young managers in Tavistock Square. While working with them he had acquired a keen interest in printing – an interest which he found that I shared. He promised to show my collection of poems to Leonard and Virginia and try to persuade them to take me on their list. At the same time, he told me that they were looking for a new manager, and that the job might include some actual printing work. Would I be prepared to be a candidate? Eagerly I said yes.

The result was that a week before Christmas I had a letter from Leonard, telling me that he and Virginia liked my book of poems very much and would be glad to publish them. He added that Dadie Rylands had told them of my interest in printing and publishing, and that they'd like to talk to me about it, as the Press was taking up more of their time than they cared to give it.

The fateful interview took place in the second week in January 1931, and immediately after I wrote to Julian in a state of exultation:

I would have written to you before about your poems, if the end of last week had not been so hectic – interviews – consultations – calculations. I expect you know substantially what the offer of the Woolves was going to be: I was surprised when they made it to me – on Friday, at tea, when I met them both for the first time, and thought them most charming, Virginia very beautiful – I was surprised and not a little excited. I've now decided I'm going to make every effort to accept the offer . . . I really can't imagine any work that would interest me more, and to be a partner with them, with a voice in what's to be published (and how) and what isn't – it seems an almost unbelievable stroke of luck.

The plans for my future at the time were either to

follow a family tradition of entering the British Diplomatic Service, or to take a post – which had been tentatively offered to me – in the Prints and Drawings Department of the British Museum. These plans now vanished like the morning mist when the sun breaks through. Looking back on the episode now, I see that it was a case of love at first sight. I had fallen head over heels in love with everything that the Hogarth Press stood for, and with Virginia Woolf in particular. Nothing could stop me in my headlong rush to accept the offer. True, there were warning voices. George Rylands for one, though on the whole pleased at the way things had turned out, reminded me of the long series of misfortunes over managers in the past, and told me that I would need to stand up for myself energetically. Julian wrote: 'Leonard has the reputation of being a very difficult employer.' Lytton Strachey, whose feelings about his old friend Leonard had a decided element of ambiguity in them, held up his hands in dismay and prophesied that I would be cunningly exploited. Perhaps he was not very serious. In any case, it was too late to daunt me. After a week of intensive consultations and calculations, with family lawyers on one side, Leonard on the other, and myself in the middle, I emerged with an agreement in my pocket by which I became manager after an eight months' apprenticeship period, and had the option of becoming a partner in two or three years. One important stipulation I made was that I should have good holidays, so that I should be able to go on writing. Leonard, an author himself, and ever sympathetic to the problems of young authors, agreed. I started at once.

In the fourth volume of his autobiography, *Downhill All the Way*, Leonard speaks only briefly, though with friendly sympathy and appreciation, of the work we did

together during this first period of my association with
the Hogarth Press; for me, it was a time of immense, and
I think decisive, significance. Leonard knew of my literary enthusiasms and of my interest in printing; he
thought he detected in me a business flair. He set about
inducting an ardently willing pupil into the mysteries of
publishing. He would come down every morning to my
cell, soon after I arrived at 9.15 a.m., with the morning's
letters in his hand. He would go through them with me
in detail, with humorous, often scathing, often illumin-
atingly reminiscent comments. He would then leave me
to answer the important letters, to design advertisements,
send books to the printers, or prepare leaflets, and to
interview all except the most distinguished callers. Generally, once a day I would go up to his study and we
would discuss the more complex problems of planning:
who to invite, for instance, to write for the various series,
such as the Hogarth Letters, which we started from time
to time, and to discuss manuscripts we had both read –
and if they were purely literary probably Virginia had
read as well.

Leonard was, in general, an extremely tolerant, broad-
minded person; but he had a number of prejudices, and
if in the course of our discussions we happened to knock
up against one of these prejudices, he would get rather
agitated, and leaning back in his chair would say: 'But,
John, it's quite *grotesque* . . .' and he would deliver his
tirade. As a self-taught publisher who had built up his
business from nothing, and as a natural sceptic, he looked
askance, even scoffingly, at many of the conventions and
sacred cows of the publishing trade. He would reduce
me to laughter as he described the anxious prudishness
and solemn ignorance of some printers, the conceit and
silliness of certain reviewers, and the impenetrable

philistinism of booksellers who *would not* make the slightest effort for anything new or experimental. He would shrug his shoulders at the apparently totally chancy ups and downs in the fortunes of books: it was irrational, and he, though the committed publisher of Freud, could not endure or even understand irrational behaviour.

I grew very fond of Leonard at that period and learned to respect his unremitting hard work, and to admire his achievements in political activity as well as in literary impresarioship. But there was shade as well as light to our association, which declared itself from the beginning. Large reverses – the failure of a book we had pinned our hopes on, the loss of the whole new printing of a book that was selling fast, in some mysterious accident – he took with philosophic calm; but quite often a small mistake in production, or a failure to account for a penny stamp in the day's petty cash, would reduce him to an absurd depth of irritation. He says himself he was a perfectionist. One may look perhaps for the cause of his insistence on the importance of small details, small money matters, in his youth in a large Anglo-Jewish family where every halfpenny counted; but I am certain that, at any rate during the years I knew him, the long nervous tension he had endured, and continued to endure, in caring so devotedly for the genius of his wife – who had in the earliest days of their marriage had a complete and terrifying mental breakdown – was responsible more than anything else. If she went out for a walk in London by herself without telling him, he would become completely distraught.

I also gradually came to learn something else about his feeling for the Hogarth Press, which was of graver import for me. Of that, more later.

My relations with Virginia at that time were brimming with an almost boundless hero-worship. In my autobiography I wrote:

At first she was irradiated in my eyes with the halo of having written *Jacob's Room*, *To the Lighthouse* and *Mrs Dalloway*. No other books seemed to me to express with anything like the same penetration and beauty the sensibility of our age; it was not merely the conception that underlay those works, of time and sorrow and human longing, but also the way she expressed it, the paramount importance in her writing of technical change and experiment; almost everything else seemed, after I had read them, utterly wide of the target and inadequately aware of what was needed. I was influenced, of course, as a poet, by the skill with which she managed to transform the material of poetry into the prose-form of the novel; but that in itself seemed to me one of the major artistic problems of our time, arising out of the terror and tension, the phantasmagoria of modern life. I devoured the three novels again and again, and always with fresh delight, valuing them far higher than *The Common Reader*, *A Room of One's Own*, *Orlando* and even *Flush*, which, much as I enjoyed them and popular as they were, seemed to me of far less significance. In those early days I revered Virginia as the sacred centre, the most gifted and adored (and sometimes feared) of the Bloomsbury circle. But, as time went on, the feeling she inspired in me was more one of happy release than of reverence. I found her the most enchanting of friends, full of sympathy and understanding for my own personal problems and the problems I was up against in my job, with an intense curiosity about my own life and the lives of my friends in my generation (many of whom were, of course, known and even related to her). She liked to hear all about what we wanted to do in poetry, in painting, in novel-writing. She would stimulate me to talk, she had an unique gift for encouraging one to be indiscreet, and would listen with absorption and occasionally intersperse pointed and witty comments.

Apart from the sessions with Leonard in his study, I would from time to time be invited up to have tea, or dinner, or drinks after dinner, with Leonard and Virginia together. There the discussions about manuscripts and publishing schemes would go on, Virginia always bubbling with ideas, many of them quite impracticable, and as I got caught up myself into her visionary flights, Leonard would often have, quietly but firmly, to pull the kites to ground. As I have said, her curiosity about people was immense, and when we weren't discussing Hogarth plans and books, she would try to pump me about mutual friends. Was it true that so-and-so had broken up his friend's marriage? Was X having a Lesbian affair with Y? Did I know anything about the latest young man Lytton Strachey was interested in? She would switch from such subjects with the easiest of transitions to discuss a new magazine, her nephew Julian's literary campaigns in Cambridge, the most recent stage production put on by the Marlowe Society, or how to deal with Hugh Walpole whose insistent devotion to her was becoming an embarrassment. Everything was grist to her mill. I do not believe there can ever have been anyone on whom the mantle of acknowledged literary fame lay less heavily.

Sometimes there were other visitors: Roger Fry, eagerly spinning his latest art theories; or Aldous Huxley, leaning in willowy length against the chimney-piece as he discoursed on recondite problems of anthropology or philosophy; or William Plomer, mocking and teasing and turning everything to absurdity; or Lytton's beautiful niece Julia, with her husband, the gifted and melancholy sculptor-poet Stephen Tomlin; and many others, luminaries and disciples of the Bloomsbury world. Virginia sat in her chair, smoking in a long holder the strong cigarettes she always rolled for herself, sometimes leading

the talk, sometimes contenting herself with brief inter-
jections, or asking questions to draw her guests out to
further confessions or declarations. I found it difficult to
take my eyes off her countenance, in which intellect,
imagination and fineness of feature were so rarely mixed.
I think of Edith Sitwell's description: 'Virginia Woolf
had a moonlit transparent beauty. She was exquisitely
carved, with large thoughtful eyes that held no fore-
shadowing of that tragic end which was a grief to everyone who had ever known her. To be in her company was
delightful. She enjoyed each butterfly aspect of the world
and of the moment, and would chase the lovely creatures,
but without damaging the coloured dust on their wings.'

Edith Sitwell, it is evident, never saw Virginia when
one of the shattering fits of fathomless, all-darkening
melancholy overcame her. Leonard Woolf has described
these crises in his autobiography, with clarity and poignancy. They began very slowly with headaches, and increasing depression. She seemed withdrawn behind a
veil, and all her gaiety and lively interest in the outside
world disappeared. Everyone in the house sensed the
accumulating tension of anxiety and distress. We knew
she was in great danger, and that Leonard was all too
keenly aware of it. These fits nearly always came on when
she was engaged on the last stages of one of her novels. It
was as if the effort of her imagination, reaching into un-
trodden regions of the mind, was beginning to crack the
delicate shell of her consciousness – of her sanity.

One of the worst of these fits attacked her as she was
writing the last pages of *The Waves*. Leonard ordered
her to abandon it altogether for a time. The crisis passed,
and she was able to complete the revision during the
summer of 1931. In her diary she wrote that she had
'reeled across the last ten pages with some moments of

such intensity and intoxication that I seemed to stumble after my own voice, or almost after some sort of speaker (as when I was mad). I was almost afraid, remembering the voices that used to fly ahead.'

Leonard Woolf has told us that after correcting the proofs she was again attacked by severe headaches and had to go to bed. Her mood of profound doubt and anxiety about the book continued. The advance copies arrived, and I seized one to read. The moment she knew this, she wrote to me: 'Lord! To think you are reading *The Waves*! Now I shall be interested to have your opinion – brutally and frankly – so please write it down for me. At present it seems to me a complete failure. And please don't tell anyone you've read it, because I'm already pestered with demands for copies, Hugh Walpole apparently having said that it's out.' And she noted, all too typically, in her diary: 'John L. is about to write to say he thinks it bad.' But John L. did not think so at all, and wrote to her with excitement and enthusiasm. So a few days later she noted in her diary that I, unlike Hugh Walpole who couldn't make head or tail of it, 'loved it, truly loved it, and was deeply impressed and amazed'. And she sat down and wrote me the following revealing letter:

I'm most grateful to you for your letter. It made me happy all yesterday. I had become firmly convinced that *The Waves* was a failure, in a sense that it wouldn't convey anything to anybody. And now you've been so perceptive, and gone so much further and deeper in understanding my drift than I thought possible that I'm immensely relieved. Not that I expect many such readers. And I'm rather dismayed to hear we've printed 7,000, for I'm sure 3,000 will feed all appetites; and then the other 4 will sit round me like decaying corpses for ever in the studio (I cleared up the table – for you, not the corpses). I agree that it's very difficult – bristling with horrors, though I've never worked so hard as I did here, to smooth them out. But it was, I think, a difficult attempt – I wanted to eliminate all detail; all fact; and analysis; and myself; & yet not be frigid and rhetorical; and not monotonous (which I am) & to keep the swiftness of prose & yet strike one or two sparks, & not with poetical, but pure-bred prose, & keep the elements of character; & yet that there should be many characters & only one; & also an infinity, a background behind – well, I admit I was biting off too much.

But enough, as the poets say. If I live another 50 years I think I shall put this method to some use, but as in 50 years I shall be under the pond, with the goldfish swimming over me, I daresay these vast ambitions are a little foolish, and will ruin the press.

In passing, I would like to draw your attention to her remark about the goldfish pond, because I think it indicates that there was a persistent undercurrent in her mind, though perhaps very deep and below the conscious, about death by drowning.

Virginia need not have worried about the sales of *The Waves*, for it was an immediate success. In the first six months after publication it sold over 10,000 in the British market and a similar amount in the American market. That meant a lot of work, rebinding and reprinting as well as an avalanche of orders to be filled every day. But I was happy, and particularly happy because I had been working at her desk which she had cleared for me. I'm afraid that one morning my curiosity got the better of my discretion, and I opened some of the drawers, which were not locked, to have a peep inside. Every drawer I opened was filled with manuscripts, half-finished sketches, short stories, critical articles and notes for future writing. Leonard has said that of the sixteen hours of her waking life, Virginia was working fifteen hours in one way or another – even when she took her walks in the countryside she was working out some writing problem, or reshaping a sentence.

In the same letter from which I have just quoted, Virginia referred to a project I had persuaded her to interest herself in. We had started a small series of Hogarth Letters, pamphlets containing about 6,000 or 7,000 words each, and I had asked Virginia, because she had begun to read the poetry of my generation with increasing curiosity, to undertake a 'Letter to a Young Poet' in the series. She wrote:

That reminds me – I think your idea of a Letter most brilliant – 'To a Young Poet' – because I'm seething with immature & ill-considered & wild & annoying ideas about prose and poetry. So lend me your name – (& let me sketch a character of you by way of frontispiece) – & then I'll pour forth all I can think of about you young, & we old, & novels – how damned they are – & poetry, how dead. But I must take a look into the subject, & you must reply, 'To an Old Novelist' – I must read Auden, whom I've not read, & Spender (his novel I swear I will tackle tonight). The whole subject is crying out for letters – flocks, volleys of them, from every side. Why not get Spender & Auden & Day Lewis to join in?

In the excitement of the appearance of *The Waves* and the first public reactions to it, and all the letters Virginia had to answer, the idea of the 'Letter to a Young Poet' did not get very much further; but Virginia was turning it over in her mind all the time. She was also changing her views about the 'deadness' of poetry, for when I sent her an inscribed copy of my first book of poems which we had just published, she wrote from their country house in Rodmell:

I am a wretch not to have thanked you for your book, which will not only stand on my shelf as you suggest but lie beneath the scrutiny of my aged eyes [she was hardly more than fifty at the time]. I want to read it with some attention, & also Auden & Day Lewis – I don't suppose there's anything for me to say about modern poetry, but I daresay I shall plunge, at your bidding. We must talk about it. I don't know what your difficulties are. Why should poetry be dead? etc., etc. But I won't run on, because then I shall spurt out my wild theories, & I've had not a moment to read for days, days – everybody in the whole world has been here. . .

As everyone knows, Virginia Woolf did plunge, and the *Letter to a Young Poet* came out in 1932. Her line was that the young poets of my generation were too introverted; wanted to publish too young; and failed in their attempt to assimilate the raw facts of life into their poetry; but mainly that they indulged too much in the sport of ranging themselves into opposing schools and movements – a habit that was much more common, traditionally, in French than in English literature.

Now of course [she wrote] writers themselves know very well that there is not a word of truth in all this – there are no battles, and no murders and no defeats, and no victories. But as it is of the utmost importance that readers should be amused, writers acquiesce. They dress themselves up. They act their parts; one leads; the other follows. One is romantic, the other realist. One is advanced, the other out of date. There is no harm in it, so long as you take it as a joke, but once you believe in it, once you begin to take yourself seriously as a leader or as a follower, as a modern or as a conservative, then you become a self-conscious, biting and scratching little animal whose work is not of the slightest value or importance to anybody. Think of yourself rather as something much humbler and less spectacular, but to my mind far more interesting – a poet in whom live all the poets of

the past, from whom all poets in time to come will spring
... in short you are an immensely ancient, complex and continuous character, for which reason please treat yourself with
respect. . .

These views were, of course, characteristic of Virginia's
profound sense of the immense antiquity and continuity
of literature; of a person who, when on the verge of insanity, heard the birds speaking *Greek* outside her window. Nevertheless, these views seemed to me to be at
variance with her own bold striking out for revolutionary
experiments a dozen years before. I think her sympathy
with what my generation was trying to do was imperfect;
a failure of sympathy which comes out more glaringly
in her later essay, *The Leaning Tower*. In a letter I wrote
to her in July, I maintained that there was no harm in
the 'dressing up' she attacked, that it was a good stimulant and was no new feature of the literary scene. She
replied at length:

Of course, dressing up may have some advantages; but not
more than gin and bitters or evening dress or any other
stimulant. Besides it becomes a habit, and freezes the elderly, like Wyndham Lewis, into ridiculous posing and pos-
turing. But it's not a matter of great importance. I admit
your next point – that is, that my quotations aren't good
illustrations; but, as usual, I couldn't find the ones I wanted,
when I was working; & was too lazy to look. Anyhow, my
impression is that I could convince you by quotations: I do
feel that the young poet is rather crudely jerked between
realism and beauty, to put it roughly. I think he is all to be
praised for attempting to swallow Mrs Gape [Mrs Gape was
the imaginary charwoman figure Virginia had introduced as
a symbol of the working class], but he ought to assimilate
her. What it seems to me is that he doesn't sufficiently believe in her; doesn't dig himself in deep enough; wakes up in

JOHN LEHMANN

the middle; his imagination goes off the boil; he doesn't
reach the unconscious, automatic state – hence the spas-
modic, jerky, self-conscious effect of his realistic language.
But I may be transferring to him some of the ill-effects of my
own struggles the other way round – with poetry in prose.
Tom Eliot I think succeeds; but then he is much more
violent; & I think by being violent, limits himself so that he
only attacks a minute province of the imagination; whereas
you younger and happier spirits should, partly owing to him,
have a greater range and be able to devise a less steep and
precipitous technique. But this is mere guesswork of course
. . . The fact is I'm not at all satisfied with the Letter, and
would like to tear up, or entirely re-write. It is a bad form for
criticism, because it seems to invite archness & playfulness,
and when one has done being playful the time's up and
there's no room for more . . .

In the same letter she adds an interesting aside : 'I
nibble at Flush, but must correct my proofs: anyhow, I
feel the point is rather gone, as I meant it for a joke with
Lytton, & a skit on him. . .'
Earlier in the year, Leonard and Virginia had taken a
holiday in Greece with Roger and Margery Fry, and left
the Hogarth Press in my hands. Virginia wrote to me
from Athens:

I have written to you several times (in imagination) a full
account of our travels, with a masterly description of Byzantine and Greek art (Roger is all for Byzantine) but I'm afraid
you never got it. The truth is it's almost impossible to put pen
to paper. . . I'm afraid you've had the devil of a time, with
Belsher away, and the doors standing open to bores of every
feather. I've often thought of you with sympathy when one
wheel of the car has been trembling over a precipice 2,000
feet deep, and vultures whirling round our heads as if sett-
ling which to begin on. . . I can assure you that Greece is
more beautiful than 20 dozen Cambridges all in May Week.

It blazes with heat too, and there are no bugs, no inconveniences – the peasants are far nicer than the company we keep in London – it's true we can't understand a word they say. In short I'm setting on foot a plan to remove the Hogarth Press to Crete. . . It has been far the best holiday we've had for years, and I feel deeply grateful to you for sitting in your doghole so stalwartly meanwhile.

Soon after they returned from Greece, I left for my own holiday abroad. I was troubled about my relations with them, as I was increasingly drawn towards Central Europe, where my friends Christopher Isherwood and Stephen Spender seemed deeply involved in the developing European crisis. What I saw of unemployment and political tension in Austria and Germany made me feel I wanted to learn more, to be present as a poet in the vortex of a coming storm. But this feeling was aggravated by the deterioration of my relations with Leonard. I learned then, what some of my predecessors in the post of assistant or manager at the Hogarth Press had surely learned before me, that the truth was that both of them, and particularly Leonard, had an emotional attitude towards the Press – as if it were the child they had never had. As the time approached when it would be my right to claim a partnership – which Leonard with half his mind desired and needed – suspicion and tension between us developed towards breaking-point. I find in my diary, towards the end of June, the following note: 'Leonard very difficult today, haggard, abrupt, twirling bits of string, a touch of hysteria in his voice, in fact suffering from severe nervous crisis, cause unknown. This manifests itself in repeated invasions of the office, anxious examinations of work being done, nagging tirades and unnecessary alarms and impatience about what is progressing steadily and in advance of the timetable.'

One might not have thought, from the tone of Virginia's letter to me from Athens, that our relations could deteriorate so sharply. But in business matters Virginia followed Leonard's lead, whatever private reservations she may have had. In any case, at the beginning of September I decided that I could not carry on at the Press, and left for abroad.

It is no part of my present story to describe the years, during the middle thirties, which I spent mainly on the continent of Europe, in Berlin, Vienna and Paris, and founded the magazine-book *New Writing*. Enough to say that, after raw wounds had healed, I maintained a certain thinned out but friendly connection with the Hogarth Press. And in the early spring of 1938 it so happened that I found myself, after two years of peddling *New Writing* between various publishers, with this brainchild, which already had a considerable reputation, on my hands again. By some curious instinct or sixth sense, while in London I suddenly felt impelled to call on Leonard and Virginia again. I had not actually seen them since my departure in 1932.

They had not tried to find another manager after I left. They were, however, tired of the drudgery of looking after the Press without any managerial help, they had kept their eyes on *New Writing*, and it would seem that they felt after all that I could be the right person to take over at least the heavier part of their responsibilities. In the most amicable discussions they offered me not only a home for *New Writing* but a resumption of my publishing career, with an excellent chance of presenting in book form the authors I was coming to find through that magazine. It was decided that after another two-year period, I should become half-owner of the Press, technically buying Virginia's share out.

The agreement came into force in April 1938, and Virginia wrote to me: 'I'm full of sanguinity about the future; and thankful to lift the burden on to your back. Nor can I see myself any reason why we should quarrel; or why we should drink the Toast in cold water. What about a good dinner (not English) at Boulestin or some such place? You are hereby invited to be the guest of Virginia Woolf's ghost – the Hogarth ghost: who rises let us hope elsewhere.'

During my first period at the Press I had been able to bring in a number of new authors, including Christopher Isherwood. Through *New Writing* I had come into contact with a great many others, both English and continental, and before long I was able to start bringing in these new poets and novelists again. Of that Leonard Woolf has written very generously in his autobiography. It is really no part of my story here to go into details, but I mention it because the interest and excitement of discovering, or often rescuing authors who had lost heart after an unappreciated start, was an important part of the pleasure and stimulus I found in working with Leonard and Virginia in those days.

It had been agreed between us that during the first year of the new arrangement I should spend some time winding up my life abroad, with the result that the outbreak of war in September 1939 arrived only a few weeks after I had returned with a car piled high with books, papers and other personal possessions from my flat in Vienna. I had not, therefore, properly worked myself in, and on that clear and beautiful September morning I felt that an evil star ruled over my publishing career. Would private publishing be possible at all under the unknown conditions of this new war? Would I be called up at once? Would London be smashed by Goering's bombers and England invaded? There was no answer at all to these insistent questions, only the gloomiest forebodings.

One day, in the first week of war, Leonard and Virginia came up from the country. They had moved themselves and the Hogarth Press from the house in Tavistock Square to a house not very far away in Mecklenburgh Square. I had taken a flat in the same square, so it was very easy for us to forgather. We ate sandwiches that day, rather despondently, in my flat, looking out at the silver barrage balloons in the sky above the plane trees. Like all of us, Virginia at that time found it extremely difficult to get rid of confused, anxious visions of the future. 'My mind seems to curl up and become undecided,' she wrote in her diary. But over the sandwiches she confessed that she was going to force herself to get on with the biography of Roger Fry upon which she had embarked, and also perhaps write some kind of autobiographical study out of all the volumes of her diary. What were we to do about the manuscripts of hopeful authors which had come in just before war was declared, which even continued to come in? They lay in their piles, like orphans without prospects, in the Hogarth basement a few doors down the row. We began to work out plans to keep the Press going somewhere, somehow, if severe bombing began.

The bombing, however, did not come to London that winter, and gradually publishing recovered from its concussion, picked itself up and dusted its coat. We had to cope with all sorts of new bureaucratic restrictions, paper rationing, staff problems. There was plenty of work to do. We began to send manuscripts to the printers again. I had signed Henry Green on, and we brought out the first of his novels under the Hogarth imprint, *Party Going*. It had enthusiastic reviews, and began to sell fast.

Leonard and Virginia were spending more time in their country house at Rodmell, and from time to time I used to go down there to discuss all our affairs. In my autobiography I wrote:

In theory I had bought Virginia out of the Press, but in fact she continued to be as keenly interested in all its activities as ever before; and every evening we would settle down in the little sitting-room upstairs, where many of the shelves were filled with books in Virginia's own fancy paper bindings, and the tables and window-sills covered with the begonias, gloxinias and rare giant lilies that Leonard raised in his greenhouses; and we would discuss books and authors and the opportunities that were open to us in the new situation. Leonard stretched out his feet towards the fire in his armchair on one side, and puffed at his pipe; Virginia on the other lit another home-rolled cigarette in her long holder. Occasional visitor only though I was, I had grown to be very fond of Monks House, the old village cottage they had bought just after the first war and rebuilt to make an ideal home for two authors to live and work in. I loved the untidy, warm, informal atmosphere of the house, with books and magazines littered about the room, logs piled up by the fireplaces, painted furniture and low tables of tiles designed by the Bloomsbury artists, and writing done in sunny, flower-filled, messy studios. A smell of wood smoke and ripe apples lingered about it, mixed with the fainter under-perfume of old bindings and old paper. We ate our meals always at the stove end of the long kitchen-scullery. . .

During those months Virginia alternated between cautious confidence and weary depression about the Roger Fry biography, very much as she always did when at work on a new book; but sometimes the depression seemed so deep that both Leonard and I encouraged her to leave it for a while, to put down on paper her objections to my generation of writers, and to prepare a third *Common Reader* collection of essays; the idea of a change nearly always lightened her mood. When *Roger Fry* was finished, however, just before Christmas, she was transformed: radiant and buoyant, full of teasing malice and the keenest interest in what her friends were doing, and finding a startling new beauty in London – the squares and side-streets in the black-out on a clear night, a transformed look in the faces of the men and women she passed – the smartness of uniforms of every sort.

As it happened, I did not read *Roger Fry* as soon as it was ready, as I would have read a new novel of hers – I had a great deal on my hands at that moment – and Virginia, I know, rather resented my silence. But my mother did read it, and wrote Virginia a letter full of praise. Virginia replied at once, with a letter in which she said: 'I only hope there will be more readers like you – anyhow, it's a great comfort to have one. I never found any piece of work so difficult. It's a bad time to bring a book out, and I'm specially sorry on John's account. It's been so hard on him, beginning his work with the war. All the same, both Leonard and I feel that the partnership is turning out a great success, at any rate from our point of view. It's years since Leonard has had such a free time. And I'm sure, when the war ends, John will make a great success of it.'

When the bombing did, finally, come to London and southern England in the summer of 1940, the first effect on Virginia was, I believe, one of exhilaration, or almost exhilaration. Leonard produced a wonderful story of a journey they made to London together, during which Virginia insisted, in a stage whisper, that a perfectly innocent nun who got into their carriage was a Nazi spy in disguise. And she wrote to me at the end of July, while the Battle of Britain was still being fought over the Sussex skies, regretting that I was prevented from coming down to see them in Rodmell: 'We could have offered you a great variety of air-raid alarms, distant bombs, reports by Mrs Bleach, who brought a stirrup pump (installed, needless to say, in my bedroom), of battles out at sea. Indeed it's rather lovely about 2 in the morning to see the lights stalking the Germans over the marshes. But this remains on tap, so you must propose yourself later. . .' I wanted to print her lecture on *The Leaning Tower* in *New Writing*, and she said in the same letter that I could indeed if she could bring herself to revise it, the idea of which she loathed. 'At the moment I can't stop reading Coleridge – thanks to you, I'm lured back to the ancients, and read a William Morris, *Chants for Socialists*, with immense pleasure. So I can't bring myself to do anything I ought to do.'

Then the bombing reached central London. The Hogarth Press building was set on fire by incendiary bombs, and further damage was caused by the floods of water directed on to it by the machines of the Fire Service. I believe a great mass of precious letters addressed to Virginia herself from innumerable correspondents, letters of a lifetime, disappeared in that fire, in that inundation. Everything that we could salvage was taken to the country, personal papers of the Woolfs to Rodmell, Hogarth Press papers to a small office which I persuaded our main printers at Letchworth on the other side of London to allow us to use.

As my own flat in Mecklenburgh Square had also been made uninhabitable in the same early September raid, I arranged to live at my family home on the Thames about thirty miles away, and made a journey, through London, to the printers and back every week. I took a temporary furnished flat in London and a small room in Cambridge, only a few miles away from the printing works. So a new rhythm of life established itself, and somehow or other, through that dislocating and disagreeable winter of fire and confusion, life, and the operations of the Hogarth Press, continued. Leonard and Virginia left the administrative side almost entirely to me – indeed they could scarcely do otherwise – and though printers and binders had more and more difficulty in fulfilling their schedules, curiously enough publishing boomed. Virginia, I understood, was at work collecting essays and articles for a third volume of *The Common Reader* – it was eventually published after her death as *The Death of the Moth* – but she was also writing something else, the work on which she had kept carefully concealed from me, and from almost everyone else except Leonard.

One day towards the middle of March, at a time when the bombing was still going on if weather favoured the bombers, Leonard and Virginia came up for the inside of the day. The three of us met for lunch at a restaurant looking out on the Houses of Parliament and Big Ben, all bathed in brilliant spring sunshine. We began to discuss a book of poems, a first book of poems by a young poet, Terence Tiller, which I had sent them. Leonard grumbled about the obscurity of the poets of my generation, but Virginia insisted that there was an unusual music and image-making power in the poems. In the end, we agreed to accept them for publication. This was the last actual book that Virginia read for the Hogarth Press.

While we were talking, I became more and more concious of the fact that Virginia seemed unusually tense and nervous, her hand shaking now and then, though she talked absolutely clearly and collectedly. It was only when we had finished Hogarth business that Leonard revealed the secret to me: Virginia had just completed – though not revised – a new novel, which had been given the title of *Between the Acts* (originally *Pointz Hall*). I was amazed, excited, immensely curious. Virginia immediately began, now rather confusedly, to say that it was no good at all, couldn't be published, must be scrapped. Very gently, but with great determination, Leonard rebuked and contradicted her, and said to me and to her that he thought it was one of the best things she had written. I pleaded to be allowed to read the typescript, and after some more argument Virginia eventually agreed to think over my eager request.

At the same time, she said that now the book was finished – she felt incapable of revision as yet – she had nothing to do. Could I help her? She jumped at my suggestion that she should read some of the manuscripts that were coming in for *New Writing*. I could not conceal from myself that there had been something desperate in her appeal.

A few days later, on 22 March 1941, the typescript arrived, and, enclosed with it, a letter from Virginia. 'I've just read my so-called novel over,' she wrote, 'and I really don't think it does. It's much too slight and sketchy. Leonard doesn't agree. So we've decided to ask you if you'd mind reading it and giving your casting vote? Meanwhile, don't take any steps. I'm sorry to trouble you, but I feel fairly certain it would be a mistake from all points of view to publish it. But as we both differ about this, your opinion would be a great help.'

I plunged into the book at once, and finished it at top speed, before I went off into the night, with my rifle and tin hat, to perform my Home Guard duty at our H.Q. near the river. I thought about it all during those wakeful hours. The first thing I had noticed was that the typing – her own typing – and the spelling were more eccentric, more irregular than in any typescript of hers I had seen before. Each page was splashed with corrections, in a way that suggested that the hand that made them had been governed by a high-voltage electric current. The second impression I had, was that the book had a quite shattering and absolutely original imaginative power, pushing her poetry – I have to call it poetry – to the extreme limits of the communicable. It was obviously in some ways unfinished, but I was deeply moved, disturbed, thrilled in the face of a revolutionary work of art.

I sent off a telegram the next morning, and followed it with a letter saying that *Between the Acts* simply must be published. As far as I was concerned, there was no question at all.

Virginia's reply came at the week-end. It wasn't what I expected:

Dear John; I'd decided, before your letter came, that I can't publish that novel as it stands – it's too silly and trivial. What I will do is to revise it, and see if I can pull it together and so publish it in the Autumn. If published as it is, it would certainly mean a financial loss; which we don't want. I am sure I am right about this.

I needn't say how sorry I am to have troubled you. The fact is it was written in the intervals of doing Roger with my brain half asleep. And I didn't realize how bad it was till I read it over.

Please forgive me, and believe I'm only doing what is best. I'm sending back the MSS [the MSS. for *New Writing*] with my notes. Again I apologize profoundly.

What was far worse was that this letter was accompanied by a letter from Leonard, in which he told me that Virginia was on the verge of one of her terrible breakdowns. Publishing the book now was out of the question. I was touched that even in the midst of this personal crisis, he could add a few words to say what bad luck it was for me as a publisher.

By the time these two letters reached me it was all over. Everyone knows the story of how Virginia Woolf drowned herself, fearing, not the war but the horrors of madness. Leonard Woolf has written a moving account of it in the last, posthumous volume of his autobiography.

It is not my intention, nor is it relevant to the story I have tried to tell, to describe the relations between Leonard and myself in the Hogarth Press after Virginia's death, our increasing disagreements – which we still disagree about after his death – and the eventual collapse of our partnership.

I would like only to conclude with what I wrote at the end of the article which I have already referred to, and which I wrote for a French literary review in 1944:

It was not the war which brought Virginia Woolf to the tragedy which ended her life. . . No, it was the strain of the task she had set herself, the dread of the fine instrument, which had created so many wonderful things already, breaking under the pressure of this last, heroic attempt. One cannot help thinking of Rhoda in *The Waves*, who cries : 'There is some check in the flow of my being; a deep stream presses on some obstacle; it jerks; it tugs; some knot in the centre resists. Oh, this is pain, this is anguish! I faint, I fail. Now my body thaws : I am unsealed, I am incandescent. Now the stream pours in a deep tide, fertilizing, opening the shut, forcing the tight-folded, flooding free. To whom shall I give all that now flows through me, from my warm, my porous body? I will gather my flowers and present them – Oh! to whom?'. . . At the end that 'knot in the centre' resisted too inexorably, and she gave her Shelleyan garland of flowers to – Death. What she might have achieved if that marvellous and still unstanched flow had broken down the 'check' once more, one can only guess; the full richness and significance of what she had already given the world is yet to be understood.

Elizabeth Bowen

(Adapted from an interview
in the BBC Television film
A Night's Darkness. A Day's Sail)

*When you think of Virginia Woolf, and remember her
appearance, does any particular image come into your
mind of what she was like?*

She was a tremendous beauty, I think that is remembered by people who knew her, but I don't know if it is realized generally. Her movements were very fluid – and when one says 'energetic' that's the wrong word, because they weren't jerky movements. She walked beautifully, when one saw her on the skyline or walking across a field. Her head was beautifully placed on her shoulders. Her hands were lovely and her movements were those of a young person. I remember somebody describing her to me before I'd seen her: I'd said, 'How does she look, what is her personality?' And they said, 'Oh, it's a spontaneous, easy and unconsciously graceful movement.' And I think one feels that in her work, in a curious way. She said to me of somebody else (I don't know whether I ought to say who it was), 'I would always know from the way she wrote that she was a beauty.' I don't think she had that in mind with regard to herself, but I think it was a very powerful factor, more than she knew, in her feeling about herself.

What did you think about her clothes?

Well, her clothes . . . as we knew, she affects in the diary

not exactly to despise them but to resent them. She *wore*
them with very great flowing charm. The first time I saw
her, which was in a garden in Bloomsbury – we were both
at a delightful tea party – she was quite at her best and
was then wearing a soft lavender muslin dress. I don't
remember her clothes well in themselves, because they
seemed merged in her. I remember this original mauvy
dress, and the hat worn forward over her face.

Was she kind to you the first time you met her?

She was extremely kind. She was formal. Describing
her to my husband when I got home, I said it was rather
like meeting the wife of a very distinguished soldier. She
wasn't one's idea of a colonel's wife, but she had this
formal, kindly, not 'condescending' air. Our conversation
was about concrete things, in fact we talked about ice-
creams – because I think there were some at the party –
and she said she was going to experiment and make green
gooseberry ones. And we talked slightly about, I suppose,
work. But she realized, I think, which was very great tact,
that I would feel it improper to tackle her about her work.
And she didn't ask condescending questions about mine,
though she appeared to know that I wrote.

Did she later on talk to you about writing?

Yes, she did. And the things she said (any of the criticisms I had from her were verbal ones. I don't remember
her writing them down) have remained with me, and I
think were extremely useful. She said, 'Don't be too
clever.' She had rather a horror of Henry James as an
influence. I don't know what she thought of Henry
James personally, but she foresaw him as a danger to me.
She said, 'Don't tie yourself up too much.' And, of a
book of mine I had sent her called *Friends and Relations*,

'It's rather spoilt for me at times, although I did enjoy it, because I feel you're like somebody trying to throw a lasso with a knotted rope.' ... Which brings me to the joy of some of the things in her Diary when she was really off-guard. Describing two or three days when she'd been a bit off her writing, she says, 'I realized I'd been riding for several days on a flat tyre.' Her wit had a way of being domestic, concrete... I still say to myself, 'Now be careful, *don't* let the rope knot!' Any faults she may have had, I don't think *her* lasso ever went into knots.

Do you think that Virginia Woolf was a genius?

I do think she was a genius. I know she was a genius. She's the only genius – as far as I know – with perhaps one exception, that I have ever sat in a room with, been familiar with, stayed in a house with, or been for a walk with. And a great deal of the time, if a person is a lovely, lively person, you just think, 'Well, they're there.' Take them for granted almost. But I do feel a conviction that something very strange that came out of her in talk, and also into her books, *was* genius.

Would it be too simple to ask you for some sort of definition of a genius, for your definition?

Some extra dimension, something that can't ever quite be accounted for in terms of aestheticism or intelligence or emotion. Something almost out of control, only it isn't. To me it comes through most strongly in *To the Lighthouse*. But also often in flashes in the Diary. And in other things I remember: her turning her head and saying – though now I can't remember the words!

There's a great deal of confusion, I think, in people's minds about whether or not Virginia Woolf was a gloomy person. It seems clear that she was melancholy, that she was – to use a medical term – manic-depressive. But equally, a whole lot of other people have nothing but stories of her gaiety and her general jollity. Did you think of her primarily as a gay person?

I was aware, one could not but be aware, of an under-tow often of sadness, of melancholy, of great fear. But the main impression was of a creature of laughter and move-ment. In the Diary she says, 'I enjoy everything I do.' Do you remember? – it was on a good day. And her power in conveying enjoyment was extraordinary. And her laugh-ter was entrancing, it was outrageous laughter, almost like a child's laughter. Whoops of laughter, if anything amused her. As it happened, the last day I saw her I was staying at Rodmell and I remember her kneeling back on the floor – we were tacking away, mending a torn Spanish curtain in the house – and she sat back on her heels and put her head back in a patch of sun, early spring sun. Then she laughed in this consuming, chok-ing, delightful, hooting way. And *that* is what has re-mained with me. So I get a curious shock when I see people regarding her entirely as a martyred . . . or de-finitely tragic sort of person, claimed by the darkness. She ended, as far as we know, in darkness, but – where is she now? Nobody with that capacity for joy, I think, can be nowhere. And it *was* joy.

What about her faults as a character? How malicious was she, do you think?

Oh, she was awfully naughty. She was fiendish. She could say things about people, all in a flash, which re-mained with one. Fleetingly malicious, rather than outright cruel. I never happened to hear her talk about anybody she really disliked or hated, so I don't know, when she unreined her furies, what it was like. But anybody who bored her or anybody absurd she was often unfair to – bless her heart! Some little fiendish phrase would fly off. And of course she was a jealous person, I think. In the realm of art she wasn't a 'competitive' person, yet I think that was a side of her that one had to watch. Sometimes her judgements were queered, I think. I was reminded sometimes of 'The Lord thy God is a jealous God: thou shalt have none other God but Me'. There was a touch of that about her occasionally. And her wit ran away with her, in some instances. She said to me about one unfortunate lady admirer who called on her, 'She thinks she looks like Shelley but actually she looks like a sugar mouse.'

What about her inquisitiveness? Do you remember any examples of that – of her consuming curiosity?

She wanted to know all the details of people's lives. That may have been because she simply wanted material. She would say to anybody, to me, or anyone to whom she was talking, 'Now what did you do, *exactly* what did you do? . . . You say you went to a party, where was it, who was there, what were they wearing?' Or, 'You walked down the street, now *why* did you walk down the street? Who were you with? What did you see? Did you see a cat, did you see a dog?' It was that sort of inquisitiveness – almost childish. I never knew her to probe *deeply* into anything, and I don't know whether she really took much interest in people's affairs of the heart or not. She never tried, as far as I was concerned, to discover anything deep down about me, or about anybody we knew in common. Past a point, her own imagination took over.

Did Virginia Woolf make fantasies about you personally?

Not as far as I know, I don't think she made fantasies about me. She would tease, of course, she would create a fantastic impression and say, 'Oh, you, when are you going back to your ancient Irish castle?' or something of that sort. She would create a fantasy to tease one about. Anything to do with the background of people fascinated her. Probably if one had lived down the bottom of a cave she would have immediately said, 'Your wonderful cave lined with pink crystal stalactites', or something of that sort. When she talked about other people to me, I've heard this fantasy thing come up. As a way of amusing herself . . . I don't know how seriously she took them. It was almost a burlesque, a love of exaggeration for its own sake.

Someone, I think it was Margery Fry, said that her sense of truth was always imaginative. Would you agree?

I would agree exactly.

What do you remember of her in society, in company?

She was less alarming, probably, in company, with several people there. She would then be as she was when I originally met her, out in that garden, rather formal. But the more frightening side of her, which some people say came out because she was frightened, I don't think it appeared so much. She seemed rather serene, rather remote. I don't know how genuine it was when she said she hated being in a room with more than a certain number of people. She must in some way have enjoyed that. Because the parties in her books, I think, are extremely enjoyable.

Did you go to many of the later Bloomsbury parties?

I went, yes. But I knew Virginia only for the last six or seven years of her life. I went to that wonderful party, which she describes, when they performed a play she wrote for her nieces and nephews to act in – Angelica Bell, for one. I spent quite a lot of evenings in her flat in London, generally with not more than a few guests in the room.

Was she in a rather excited state during the parties?

She was, I think. She was keyed up. But she was always in perfect command. I mean, she wasn't sort of foolishly keyed up. Nonetheless, one could feel a certain state of intensity. Or she would start that terrible game when she teased people. She used to love teasing dear Tom Eliot, whom she was absolutely devoted to, and he used to love that. But she said to him once, 'It's such a pity, Tom, that you started being a poet instead of remaining in a bank. By now you might have been the Manager of the Bank of England.' He looked rather taken aback, but on the whole pleased. He purred like a very serious cat. If she was fond of people, she just wanted to make a little fun, and intrigue them, and amuse other people. She was incapable of keeping up a purely formal conversation for a long time. On the whole, society had a neutralizing effect on her. When I was alone with her I used to have, at first, a feeling of awe and alarm. As a rule, that wore off. But sometimes she seemed tired, or extra remote.

Angus Davidson

MY first contacts with the so-called 'Bloomsbury Group' were made, through Maynard Keynes, when I was an undergraduate at Cambridge in the early twenties. Maynard, already a distinguished economist, though the days of his greatest fame were to come later, had a discerning enthusiasm for painting: he not only acquired a large number of French Impressionist pictures, but his rooms in King's, where he was generous and charming in his entertaining of undergraduates, were decorated with splendid panels by Vanessa Bell and Duncan Grant. It was there that I first met these two painters, who were afterwards to be numbered among my dearest friends. In London they shared a house in Gordon Square with Maynard, in the country there was Charleston, an old Sussex farmhouse under the Downs near Lewes, which had been discovered by Vanessa Bell, on a bicycle, and taken over by her in a fairly primitive state. Maynard Keynes was a frequent visitor there (until his marriage, later, to Lydia Lopokova, when he moved into Tilton, about half a mile away) and in the summer, especially, Clive and Vanessa Bell and the children would all be there, and Duncan Grant. The Woolfs, then living in Tavistock Square, had a house at Rodmell, not very far away. Of my first meeting with Leonard and Virginia I have no precise recollection; it must have been either at Gordon Square or at Charleston, where I often used to stay and where I still go quite often to see Duncan Grant, the only survivor, now, of the group.

All these people, already distinguished and fifteen or twenty years older than myself, were somewhat alarming, at first, to a rather diffident young man. It was a great pleasure – and, one felt, a great privilege – to be with them and to listen, even if one did not contribute much, to their conversation. They had the art of discussing important matters, whether aesthetics, literature, philosophy or religion, with a combination of seriousness and intellectual penetration and, on the other hand, lightness and humour – or even ribaldry – which removed all dullness or stodginess from even the weightiest subjects. Virginia, with her brilliant mind and natural wit – she had a gift of effortless 'style' in her talk as in even the least important of her writings – had great charm and a perfectly unselfconscious personal beauty which she did nothing to enhance artificially. She could make very cutting remarks, but seldom, I think, with real bitterness: there was an underlying humour, an irony, that saved them from being truly malicious. This, indeed, was a sort of Bloomsbury 'game', in which Lytton Strachey, one of her closest friends, was perhaps the supreme champion, and which has not been sufficiently understood by people, writers included, who never knew them personally and who have taken their sharp remarks too seriously.

There were gatherings at Gordon Square (several of the Strachey family were living almost next door) and at the Woolfs' flat round the corner in Tavistock Square, at which one met such eminent figures as E. M. Forster, Lytton Strachey, Aldous Huxley, T. S. Eliot (shy and quiet but with a charming manner), the formidable composer Dame Ethel Smyth (tweeds and a Homburg hat) and, occasionally, Victoria Sackville-West; but she, a devoted friend and admirer of Virginia, came seldom to London, preferring life in the country and her garden. At one of the gay parties in Gordon Square the success of the evening was Berta Ruck, a novelist well known in a milieu rather different from Virginia's: the latter, in one of her novels, had quite unwittingly placed Miss Ruck's name on a tombstone (I suppose she had registered it unconsciously from some review or advertisement), and Miss Ruck wrote to her in sorrow and indignation. However, all was eventually forgiven: Miss Ruck was invited to the party, where she delighted everyone by singing, with mellow abandon, a slightly bawdy song: 'Never allow a sailor an inch above your knee.'

It must have been about this time (in 1924) that Leonard and Virginia invited me to come and work at the Hogarth Press, which had been started when they lived at Richmond but had now moved to the basement at Tavistock Square, below the Woolfs' flat. I was to succeed Dadie Rylands who, having won a fellowship at King's, Cambridge, was leaving to become a don. I was delighted at this offer. I pictured myself reading manuscripts and discussing them with Leonard and Virginia and working at last in a job which, since I myself had ambitions as a writer and was already doing reviewing and a certain amount of art criticism, would be really interesting to me. But though I stayed there for nearly five years, things did not turn out quite as I had hoped. In the literary side of the Press I had scarcely any share. Leonard – consulting, presumably, with Virginia – kept this entirely to himself: my opinion was never asked. Apart from a little occasional printing on the hand-press in the back room of the basement (the former scullery of the house), my duties were not much more than those of an office-boy. My impression, forty-five years later, is that they consisted mainly in doing up endless parcels and making out invoices and bills, and an occasional round of 'travelling' the London bookshops to get orders for books that were about to appear. And Leonard, charming, intelligent, efficient and of absolute integrity, was nevertheless not easy to work with. He insisted on keeping everything in his own hands: one was told what to do and there was no discussion. Moreover, he was extremely irritable, and his perpetually shaking hands seemed to emphasize this. He was a stickler for absolute punctuality. I was supposed to arrive at the office at half past nine in the morning, and living, as I did, not very far off, this should not have been difficult. But, inevitably, there were mornings when I was two or three minutes late and would find Leonard fuming, a bundle of papers in his hand, looking at his watch. There was one absurd occasion when our watches varied by two minutes; and we ran out up the basement steps together to look down the street at the immense clock that projected above the door of Pitman's School in Russell Square. It was only later that I realized that this extreme nervous irritability must have been largely due to the great strain imposed upon him by Virginia's illnesses.

But Virginia, by that time, was better: the worst of her attacks had taken place earlier. She still suffered, at times, from severe headaches and would disappear for two or three days; but most of her time was spent in her workroom. This was a vast and gloomy place, originally built, I imagine, as a billiard-room. To reach it one went out by the back door of the basement and along a narrow passage. The room had no windows, only a top light, and was infinitely austere: a table or two, a chair, a few shelves.

It was like being at the bottom of a tank or well, and in some people it might well have caused claustrophobia. Few people, I think, were permitted to penetrate into it. She took little part in the running of the Press. By this time very little printing was done on the premises. This had been started at Richmond – so I understood – as a sort of treatment, a sedative, for Virginia, who enjoyed setting up type and found it soothing, but as her health grew better and the number of books published increased, it was gradually given up and the printing was done by professional firms. She would come into the office occasionally, if there was a rush of work, and help, not very efficiently, to do up a few parcels, and this she enjoyed. The whole atmosphere lightened when it happened. She would talk and be gay and amusing, and it was always a pleasure to see her, with her look of great distinction even in the most ordinary, rather nondescript, everyday clothes. (She seemed, on the whole, to have little interest in clothes, certainly not in conventional fashions, but, with her tall, slim figure, could achieve considerable elegance when she was going out in the evening. And always distinguished, always an individual, unlike anybody except her sister Vanessa.) And when she talked, in her unusually pleasing voice, she had a way of describing even the most ordinary things that made them seem interesting and funny.

Between the two sisters there was a marked physical resemblance. A resemblance, also, in vigour of mind, in wit, in charm and distinction and sense of humour. (But Vanessa taking off Lady Ottoline Morrell, a not very popular figure in Bloomsbury circles, was inimitable: and this was a thing one could not imagine Virginia attempting.) Much of the difference in their attitude to life may have been due to Vanessa's having produced a family. She was more calm and composed, also more practical: she sewed beautifully, she was a good driver, she could cook if required, whereas I don't believe Virginia did any of these things. But then she had maids, the admirably competent Nellie and Lottie (I am thinking of the Tavistock Square days). I have often wondered whether, if she had had children, it would have stabilized her. Leonard, I am sure, would have been a very good father, but it is hard to imagine Virginia as a mother. Devoted, certainly, and indulgent, but perhaps in a rather intermittent fashion. I think that at times children would have exasperated her. But she was on the closest terms of friendship (with little of the 'aunt' about it) with Vanessa's children, Julian and Quentin and Angelica.

One of Virginia's greatest pleasures was travelling abroad. This, as Leonard remarks in his autobiography, 'had a curious and deep effect upon her... She fell into a strange state of passive alertness. She allowed all these foreign sounds and sights to stream through her mind' and 'months afterwards [they] would become food for her imagination and her art ... A mixture of exhilaration and relaxation'. Something of this is shown in a letter she wrote to me when they were in Sicily in 1927. 'We are both burnt bright brick red,' she wrote from Syracuse, 'we are both slightly tipsy. We are almost decided never to come back to England again... Happily we have pitched on a purely Italian inn – rather humble; w.c.'s fair; no English spoken, and we sit drinking coffee with Italian sailors and officers after dinner. We have been all day ... among the ruins of the Greek theatre, where they are getting up a play to act next week before the King and Queen; so we saw Medea in a sulphur-coloured wig and Alcestis [but it could not have been Alcestis!] in a bowler and overcoat, shouting their parts. It was rather beautiful.' But soon their mode of travel changed. They bought a second-hand car which already had an old-fashioned, rather dowdy look and which Vita Sackville-West unkindly nicknamed 'The Old Umbrella'. It served its purpose very well, however, and in 1928 took them without disaster to Cassis in the South of France, where Clive and Vanessa Bell and Duncan Grant were staying in a small villa. 'Everyone here is as odd as usual,' Virginia wrote to me from there; 'Julian has actually made himself sick laughing at Duncan and me. Our eccentricities seem to flower in the South, and the frogs keep talking incessantly... The Singer runs so fast on French roads that we got here early. It is undoubtedly what one will do in Heaven – motoring all day, and eating vast meals, and drinking red wine and liqueurs.'

At Rodmell, and at Charleston too, there was gaiety and laughter, especially when Julian and Quentin were there – Clive Bell with his boisterous guffaws, Vanessa sitting quietly attentive and putting in an occasional dry comment, Virginia with her mocking wit and Duncan with his vagueness and his entertaining (and of course largely assumed) dottiness – these last two acting as ideal foils to one another. Staying for a week-end at Rodmell, as I did more than once, was a great pleasure. Virginia was a charming hostess and, unlike some hostesses, had the sensible habit of leaving one a good deal to oneself. She herself would probably be working and would disappear for a good part of the day into her hut at the far end of the orchard. There was the lovely garden which Leonard, an expert, had created, and there one would sit reading, or go for walks down into the valley. In the evenings, after dinner, we would sit talking, Virginia smoking a cheroot. These were the long, thin cheroots which came in little bundles of six or eight, and she would give me one. And then, as I was leaving, she gave me a complete bundle. I have always remembered that generous, thoughtful gesture: she knew that I liked them and that, being far from rich, I would not buy them for myself.

Virginia would often speak of Cornwall, a region which, for her, had a very special, almost magical quality. She had spent many summer holidays there as a child, in the house which her father owned at St Ives, and she and Leonard had been down there more than once, staying, generally, with the Arnold-Forsters at Zennor (Ka Arnold-Forster, as Ka Cox, had achieved fame as the intimate friend of Rupert Brooke). 'I always feel,' Virginia wrote to me, 'that I am the original owner of Cornwall, and everyone else is a newcomer. But you will excuse this peculiarity.' This was after I myself had gone to live there during the last years before the war, and there was an occasion, ever to be regretted, when they came to see me in my cottage at Sennen, and I, alas (they had not warned me beforehand), was not there. It was her love of the district that had given rise to *To the Lighthouse*, the setting of which is the house at St Ives, and the Godrevy Lighthouse, visible from the house; and two of the characters are portraits of her father and mother. The Arnold-Forsters' house at Zennor was a strange place, perched high up among the rocks above the sea. 'It is bitterly cold,' Virginia wrote to me from there. 'We are motored over the moors to Land's End and other remote places. We look down into the heart of the Atlantic from our bedroom. All my facts about lighthouses are wrong.' Like her elm trees in the Hebrides, perhaps!

One of Virginia's closest friends at this time was Vita

Sackville-West, who, in turn, had a great admiration for Virginia. My impression was that Virginia looked upon this distinguished, if rather formidable woman – a remarkable poet and novelist and creator of gardens – as a kind of rock upon which she could lean when in trouble, a stable character with a strong practical sense and with a touch of masculinity about it, a contrast to her own volatile, vulnerable nature. Vita was essentially a 'country' person: she had a deep love and an exhaustive historical knowledge of Knole, the vast and splendid house which had been her home and which, if she had been a man, she would have inherited, together with the Sackville title. In those days she and her husband, Harold Nicolson, lived near by, and Leonard and Virginia would visit her there, or she would go to Rodmell. This happened especially at the time (about 1927) when Virginia was engaged in the writing of that curious and fascinating book *Orlando*, of which Vita was the heroine-hero. Vita seldom went to London: she was by no means a social or sociable person, though evidently she had a gift for intimate friendships with women. Another of her devoted friends – a friend of Virginia's also, though not on such close terms – was Dorothy Wellesley (later Duchess of Wellington), a woman of great charm and a poet of distinction, who lived in a beautiful house near Withyham in Sussex and whose garden Vita had helped to design. I recall this garden on a brilliant spring day, with an avenue of dazzling cherry trees in pink blossom and beds of bright wallflowers below them.

'Sociable' Vita was not – less so, I should say, than Virginia, who had a great interest in people and was not averse to making new acquaintances. She might be bored by them, but obviously enjoyed speculating upon them afterwards and sometimes would invent characters for them which were not necessarily accurate. It was Vanessa who was the unsociable one, at any rate in her later years, when, except for her own family and intimate friends, she became rather a hermit. She had very definite likes and dislikes. Casual visitors were not welcome. If she could, she avoided them; if not, she was perfectly polite but not encouraging. The death of her elder son, Julian, in the Spanish Civil War, affected her profoundly and perhaps to some extent altered her attitude to the outside world. But she could still be gay and amusing and immensely charming among her old and intimate friends. Among these was Roger Fry, who was often staying at Charleston in the years before the war. Virginia's Life of him (the only straightforward biography she wrote – *Orlando* and *Flush* can hardly be counted as such) was, to my mind, her least successful work. As an assemblage of facts and events it is thorough and admirable; but perhaps it allowed too little scope for her radiant imagination; perhaps she was too close to him to achieve the detachment that is desirable in an ideal biographer.

After Virginia's death in 1941 Leonard settled down to a quiet, solitary life at Rodmell. After the first terrible times of shock I think he was not unhappy. He continued with his political work, going quite often to London; he maintained his direction of the Hogarth Press, now linked with the firm of Chatto & Windus; he had his sheepdogs and his Siamese cats; above all, he took an ever-increasing and more and more expert pleasure in his garden, a lovable place, part of which is divided into compartments surrounded by the low, ruined walls of ancient buildings. But the most important thing to him now was the writing of his autobiography, that fascinating work in five volumes which deserves all the praise and success it has had. Although he had produced several books before this, largely political, and an excellent novel about Ceylon, *The Village in the Jungle*, he had never, before his wife's death, put himself forward as a writer, in spite of his great gifts in that field. He is extremely frank, in the autobiography, on the painful subject of Virginia's breakdowns and of the terrible nervous strain they caused.

I believe I was one of the last people to see Leonard before he died. He had already had a second stroke, but I was allowed to go and sit with him for a short time. It was a sad, strange, difficult conversation: he could, I think, understand everything I said, but when he tried to answer he was unable to find the right words, so that his replies were irrelevant and often incomprehensible. But he seemed pleased to see me. It was a warm summer day and we sat in the garden, looking across the lovely valley of the Ouse, the river which, some twenty-eight years earlier, had been the scene of Virginia's unhappy end.

Rosamond Lehmann

THOSE who knew Virginia Woolf well will speak and write of her as the woman she was in daily domestic life – a life outwardly uneventful, devoid of publicity, blessed by a few close friendships and by a love that cared for and supported her from first to last. But for those, such as myself, whose meetings with her were infrequent, she was bound to preserve intact a quality of poetic significance which colours, sharpens, perhaps distorts her figure in memory.

Many good poets have been prose figures, with their genius locked away in a separate compartment; but she was in herself, in her person, a perfectly poetic creature. There was no process of readjustment to go through on seeing her, no disappointment to overcome. The only surprise was to find a human being so all of a piece without and within; one who so clearly expressed her spirit in her body. She was extremely beautiful, with an austere intellectual beauty of bone and outline, with large melancholy eyes under carved lids, and the nose and lips, the long narrow cheek of a Gothic madonna. Her voice, light, musical, with a throaty note in it, was one of her great charms. She was tall and thin, and her hands were exquisite. She used to spread them out to the fire, and they were so transparent one fancied one saw the long fragile bones through the fine skin. She dressed like an aesthetic don. There was something about her that made one think of William Morris and the New Age and the Emancipation of Women.

Her conversation was a brilliant mixture of reminiscence, gossip, extravagantly fanciful speculation and serious critical discussion of books and pictures. She was malicious, and she liked to tease. Now and then her tongue had a corrosive edge, and one suspected that she enjoyed the embarrassment and discomfiture of a victim. She delighted to draw people out, plying them with questions, riotously embroidering upon what they told her, and generally suggesting to them a conception of themselves as leading lives of superlative interest and originality. To her friends she was the soul of sympathy and understanding.

She was very quiet, rather slow, not graceful, in her movements, economical in her gestures; yet she gave an impression of quivering nervous excitement, of a spirit balanced at a pitch of intensity impossible to sustain without collapse. One felt that she had to guard herself against the attack of humanity; that the pressure of other people upon her might at any moment become too painful and shatter her in pieces. She loved jokes, cracked them herself without decorum, and laughed at those of others. She enjoyed praise and was terribly sensitive to misunderstanding or adverse criticism; but fundamentally she had complete artistic humility and sincerity, and was never satisfied with what she had accomplished. Nobody was ever less arrogant, spoilt or vulgar.

She had her share of griefs and bore them with courage and unselfishness. It is important to say this in view of the distasteful myths which have risen around her death: the conception of her as a morbid invalid, one who 'couldn't face life', and put an end to it out of hysterical self-pity. No. She lived under the shadow of the fear of madness; but her sanity was exquisite.

She never grew accustomed, she never dried up. It is impossible to imagine her ceasing to be able to make poetry out of experience. One epitaph might be that there was something better than she had ever done which she could still, even in old age, have done. There was never an end to the meanings within meanings that memories and characters and any ordinary event or spectacle contained for her. A family meal, a walk by the seashore, the crowds passing in the street, a young man returning to his college rooms at night, a woman carrying a baby, the flying arc cut by a bird's wing, a fin turning in a waste of waters – all are seen, not as objects in themselves alone, but lit in all directions by flashes of symbolic and spiritual meaning. What human beings did, their everyday material occupations and professions, the surface means by which they communicated, had for her less reality than the underside of them – their mysteriousness, their bewildering and inapprehensible destiny : 'as if time and eternity showed through skirts and waistcoats, and she saw people passing tragically to destruction'.

Although she never used a difficult or an obscurantist expression, though her dialogue is so simple as almost to seem written for a child, and the total impression is of something said or sung in a voice of piercing lucidity, the underlying structure of her novels defies a strict analysis. Visions of the passage of time run through them, visions of perpetual change and flux, of chaos cohering suddenly into a centre of order and stability, an abstract shape of peace. She was intensely aware of the spiritual reality of human beings. All we can see of them, she seems to say, is the luminous and iridescent haze surrounding the dark score. Then all at once she causes this haze to become incandescent; and there, over and over again, darkly burning within their haloes, appear Jacob, Mrs Dalloway, Mrs Ramsay, Percival, fixed in lasting moments of youth and age, of beauty and love, of happiness and pathos; focusing and embodying the continuity of life and its inscrutable meaning.

What is life? What is meaning? Her work is a perpetual exploration with this question like a lamp held up above the theme. Unwaveringly vigilant, she bends the lamp here and there upon complexity and paradox; suggesting, so it seems, precisely this, her method, as a clue to the proper function of human consciousness: saying it is experiment and search, is a preparation for the unexpected, the unknown; a leap any day, in any place, at any age, from a pinnacle into the elements of darkness. Her voice is both austere and ecstatic; stoical in the face of death, which she saw as ineluctable annihilation, yet constantly affirming: 'Life! More life!'

Perhaps it is impossible to attempt to build a bridge between Virginia Woolf and the 'average man'. Certainly when he asserts that normal people don't go on and on asking what is the meaning of life and shying off from any definite conclusion, that such an attitude is unwholesome, absurd, that it gets you nowhere, one can only reply: 'Yes, she was far from normal, and what she had to say helps nobody to get on in the world. She wasn't at all tough, she quite lacks the cheery common-sense point of view and there's no plot or story in her novels.'

But there is another attack, equally truculent and self-righteous, and more dogmatic, which descends upon her; and against criticism of this type it is a duty to protest, because it is an attack upon culture in the name of culture. In a number of a publication of the Left, in the course of an article consigning to wholesale perdition or oblivion most of the better-known English writers of our time on the grounds that they have 'consistently rejected history' I read: 'Virginia Woolf, the outstanding prose writer of the English Twilight of individual subconsciousness, has accepted the judgement of history and taken the logical step.' Leaving aside the questionable taste of this bland statement one is obliged to ask: Whose history? Is one political party alone to identify itself with history and pronounce verdicts against which there can be no appeal? Are the values of art henceforth to be rigidly geared to the development of class war, and imaginative sensibility to be assessed exclusively in terms of 'political consciousness'? Surely the hand that so arbitrarily and complacently sweeps away 'outworn' culture in the name of 'history' bears a disquieting resemblance to the hand that reaches for its revolver at the very mention of culture. And surely, not to speak out upon this issue, for her sake, for her art's sake, and in the name of that very 'idea of change which is the beginning of revolution' – an idea to which she was as receptive and sympathetic as any poet of her generation – would indeed be the descent of the English Twilight.

It is true that there was much which she lacked, much which was outside the scope of her powers. She was not equipped for a broad grasp of humanity, she had not the kind of richness and sanity, the rooted quality which comes from living a completely fulfilled life as a woman and a mother. She had a romantic view of charwomen and prostitutes; and her conception of the ruling classes, of rank, fashion, titles, society – all that – was perhaps a shade glamorous and reverential. Then, as regards her technique: she had two styles, one clear, logical and concise, an admirable instrument for her admirable critical prose; the other for her imaginative work, a poetic style, full of light, flexible, expanded rhythms; and this, in spite of its brilliance and beauty, has moments when it irritates, when one detects tricks, when it seems too airy, giddy almost; a trifle archly hesitant. In spite of the extraordinary loveliness of her images, there are moments when the quivering antennae of her senses seem too receptive, and almost stifle one with minute impressions. Blinds sway, brooms tap, chairs creak too frequently. Also there are moments, particularly in *The Waves*, when her sense of the duality in human consciousness – the I for ever watching the I – gives one an uneasy feeling of a neurotic split in personality. This split has penetrated deeper far into her last novel *Between the Acts*. When I first read it I found it very upsetting in that it appeared to me the product of a mind on the verge of breakdown, or fatally fatigued. It is a very dark book, imbued with images of destruction and disintegration. I do not share the admiration most critics accord to it.

But when all this is said, to re-read *Jacob's Room, Mrs Dalloway, To the Lighthouse, The Waves* is to recapture a vision of life of enchanting freshness, of deepening poignancy and profundity. To my mind, it is in *To the Lighthouse* that she grasped and expressed it with the greatest sweep and lyrical ecstasy, the most moving imagery. There is not one paragraph that flags or falters; and it contains more human love, grief and happiness than do any others of her books. Even so, the one that I now re-read with the greatest enjoyment is the posthumously published *A Writer's Diary*. I find it the most illuminating and enriching of them all.

In another sphere, the last work to be published in her lifetime, the biography of Roger Fry, is her masterpiece. The best powers of her intellect and her emotions went to the making of it; and it is remarkable no less for its solid sense of form than for its background of an age and a way of life, and for the roundness, warmth and depth of its central portrait. Here, in this life of her friend, we see, unshadowed by hesitations and withdrawals, the firm values by which she lived: the values of art, of learning and of personal relationships.

Clive Bell

I WANT in this attempt to describe Virginia to dispel certain false notions. One result of the publication of extracts from her diary (*A Writer's Diary*, Hogarth Press) has been to confirm an opinion already current, the opinion that Virginia's nature was harsh and unhappy. Nothing could be farther from the truth. Yet, though the inference drawn from the published diaries is false it would be excusable had not the editor, Mr Leonard Woolf, been at pains to put readers on their guard. On the very first page of his preface he writes: 'At the best and even unexpurgated, diaries give a distorted or one-sided portrait of the writer, because, as Virginia Woolf herself remarks somewhere in these diaries, one gets into the habit of recording one particular kind of mood – irritation or misery say – and of not writing one's diary when one is feeling the opposite. The portrait is therefore from the start unbalanced, and, if someone then deliberately removes another characteristic, it may well become a mere caricature.'

Someone did remove another characteristic. The editor, himself, very properly cut out a number of passages which were much too personal, not to say libellous, to be published while the victims were alive.

Despite this warning, there are those who find confirmation in these diaries of what they wish to believe and retell the old tale – Virginia Woolf was gloomy and querulous; so I will add a few sentences to what her husband has said clearly enough. More often than not the diary was written in moments of agitation, depression or nervous irritation; also the published extracts are concerned almost entirely with her work, a subject about which she never felt calmly. Indeed, creating a work of art, as the diary shows, was for Virginia a cause, not only of moral but of physical exasperation – exasperation so intense that often it made her positively ill. I should not be surprised if some lively journalist had dubbed the book 'Screams from the torture-chamber', for truly much of it must have been written when the author felt much as one feels at the worst moments of toothache. Even so, were the unpublished part (the published is not a twentieth of the whole) before the reader, it is certain that his idea of the writer would change completely. Of this unpublished part I know only scraps; and even these will not be printed for some years I surmise. Nor can I choose but rejoice; for amongst pages of gay and brilliant description will be found many disobliging comments on the sayings and doings and characters of her friends – of whom I was one. Wherefore here and now I should like to interpose a caution. Those comments and descriptions, those that I have read or heard read, though always lively and amusing are not always true.

Sooner or later Virginia's diaries and letters will be printed. They will make a number of fascinating volumes: books, like Byron's letters, to be read and re-read for sheer delight. In the midst of his delight let the reader remember, especially the reader who itches to compose histories and biographies, that the author's accounts of people and of their sayings and doings may be flights of her airy imagination. Well do I remember an evening when Leonard Woolf, reading aloud to a few old friends extracts from these diaries, stopped suddenly. 'I suspect,' said I, 'you've come on a passage where she makes a bit too free with the frailties and absurdities of someone here present.' 'Yes,' said he, 'but that's not why I broke off. I shall skip the next few pages because there's not a word of truth in them.'

That Virginia possessed the poet's, and dreamer's faculty of 'making Cables of Cobwebbes and Wildernesses of handsome Groves' will surprise no one who has read her books; what may surprise is that she should have employed this faculty not only in art but in life. I have gone so far as to conjecture – and it was going rather far I admit – that at times she saw life and to some extent experienced it as a novel or rather as a series of novels, in which anyone of her friends might find him or herself cast, all unawares, for a part. Yours might be a sympathetic role, and in that case all you said and did would be seen through roseate lenses, your banal comments would be transmuted to words of wisdom or subtle intuition, your ungainly gestures would acquire an air of dignity and significance. Sometimes, however – in my case generally – it was quite the other way. But for better or for worse one's character, conduct and conversation had to fit in to a picture which existed in the artist's imagination. To one's surprise, often to one's dismay, one found oneself the embodiment of a preconceived idea.

I felt so sure that there was something in my theory that I propounded it to one of Virginia's friends, from whom I heard a story to confirm my suspicions. This friend happened to be a lady, elegant and aristocratic to be sure, but unconventional to the verge of eccentricity. Her manners certainly were all that manners should be;

but she was a rebel at heart, and her conversation and way of life would have shocked her mother profoundly and did shock her more sedate relations. No one could have been less like a leader of Victorian society. Nevertheless, in one of those marvellous romances which were a part of Virginia's everyday existence, that is what this wayward individual – Lady X shall we call her? – had to be: the typical leader of rather old-fashioned 'Society', exquisite and soignée (as she was) but also classically correct, smooth and sure of herself, running true to form in a world of dukes, ambassadors and orchids. To give a sharper point to this imaginary relationship – the friendship of a *grande dame* and a novelist – Virginia, who besides being one of the most beautiful was one of the best-bred women of her age, cast herself in the role of a tough, uncouth, out-at-elbows Bohemian – of genius. And such was the spell she threw, such the cogency of her imagination, that many a time poor Lady X found herself, not only playing up to the role assigned to her, but positively accepting Virginia in the role she had allotted to herself. Am I not justified, then, in beseeching a vast posterity of enchanted readers to be on their guard?

To return for a moment to that silly caricature – Virginia the gloomy malcontent – let me say once and for all that she was about the gayest human being I have known and one of the most lovable, I was going to add 'besides being a genius'; but indeed these qualities were elements of her genius: in that sense she was all of a piece. I am not suggesting that she was faultless, or that those who have suspected her of being a little jealous on occasions or unwilling to 'brook a rival near the throne' were merely malevolent gossips. Only her jealousies and lapses of sympathy were of such a peculiar kind that it is difficult to understand them and easy to exaggerate. I do not pretend to understand them entirely, and so will give an example or two, leaving the reader to provide his own explanation. Someone said in her presence that it must be very tiring for her sister, a painter, to stand long hours at the easel. Virginia, outraged, I suppose, by the insinuation that her sister's occupation was in any way more exacting than her own, went out at once and bought a tall desk at which she insisted on standing to write. But this was when she was very young, and the very young are apt to be touchy. Surely she was guilty of excessive touchiness when she complained – a friend having told her I had said in a letter that she was looking well (she had been ill) – that 'Clive thinks I have become red and coarse'. It was a sort of jealousy, no doubt, that made her deprecate her friends pursuing the arts or professions which seemed in some way to put them in competition with herself. From time to time she would regret that Duncan Grant had not accepted a commission in the Black Watch – 'I feel sure he would have been a remarkable soldier' (so do I). I believe she herself felt that she had gone a little far when she told me that Lytton Strachey should have been an Indian civil servant; but perhaps she was right when she persuaded Molly MacCarthy to write me a letter (to which I replied beginning 'Dearest Virginia') pointing out that critics were mere parasites on art and that my abilities (such as they were) would be much better employed at the bar. I think there was a sort of jealousy in all this, but I also think there was a sort, a very odd sort, of Victorianism. Sometimes it seemed to me that Virginia had inherited from her immediate ancestors more than their beauty and intelligence. Every good Victorian knew that a young man should have a sensible profession, something solid and secure, which would lead naturally to a comfortable old age and a fair provision for the children. In her head Virginia knew perfectly well that to give such advice to Lytton or Duncan was absurd; but Virginia, like the merest man, was not always guided by reason.

I said 'the merest man' because Virginia was, in her peculiar way, an ardent feminist. What is more, some of her injustices and wanton denigrations can be traced, I think, to female indignation. In political feminism – the Suffrage Movement – she was not much interested, though I do remember that once or twice she and I went to some obscure office where we licked up envelopes for the Adult Suffrage League. But, as you will have guessed, it was not in political action that her feminism expressed itself: indeed she made merciless fun of the flag-wagging fanaticism of her old friend Ethel Smyth. What she minded most, perhaps, was what she considered male advantages, and especially advantages in education. Readers of *A Room of One's Own* will remember an amusing but none the less bitter, comparison of lunch in King's with dinner at Girton; and intelligent readers will have felt that the comparison is to be carried a great deal farther. Also she resented the way in which men, as she thought, patronized women, especially women who were attempting to create works of art or succeed in what were once considered manly professions. Assuredly Virginia did not wish to be a man, or to be treated as a man: she wished to be treated as an equal – just possibly as a superior. Anyhow the least suspicion of condescension irritated her intensely and understandably. She grew angry and lashed out; and her blows fell, as often as not, on innocent noses. She could be monstrously, but delightfully, unfair; and witty blows below the belt sometimes leave nasty bruises. Neither male nor female can be wholly objective about *Three Guineas*, but for my part I feel sure it is her least admirable production.

Virginia's feminism was genuine and ardent, yet I do not think it played a great part in her life. Certainly the tantrums to which it gave rise were rare and transitory; and I will make bold, and bold it is, to say that hers was a happy nature. I know all about those fits of black despair; she had something to be desperate about, seeing that the threat of collapse always hung over her if she indulged too freely her ruling passion – the passion to create. Writing was her passion and her joy and her poison. Yet, I repeat, hers was a happy nature and she was happy. As for her gaiety – does this seem significant? My children, from the time they were old enough to enjoy anything beyond their animal satisfactions, enjoyed beyond anything a visit from Virginia. They looked forward to it as the greatest treat imaginable: 'Virginia's coming, what fun we shall have.' That is what they said and felt when they were children and went on saying and feeling to the end. And so said all of us. So said everyone who knew her. 'What fun we shall have' and what fun we did have. She might be divinely witty or outrageously fanciful; she might retail village gossip or tell stories of her London friends; always she was indescribably entertaining; always she enjoyed herself and we enjoyed her. 'Virginia's coming to tea': we knew it would be exciting, we knew that we were going to laugh and be surprised and made to feel that the temperature of life was several degrees higher than we had supposed...

I remember spending some dark, uneasy, winter days, during the first war in the depths of the country with Lytton Strachey. After lunch, as we watched the rain pour down and premature darkness roll up, he said, in his searching, personal way, 'Loves apart, whom would you most like to see coming up the drive?' I hesitated a moment, and he supplied the answer: 'Virginia of course.'

Frances Marshall

(Mrs Ralph Partridge)

SOON after I came down from Cambridge in the early twenties I took my first paid job in the bookshop that had been started by Francis Birrell and David Garnett. It was in a house off Gordon Square and the clientele was almost exclusively Bloomsburian. The 'Woolves' were among the customers, though not very frequent ones; but at this time Ralph Partridge was working for the Hogarth Press, travelling their books, and he came to see us on their behalf. When we moved later to the grander, more shop-like premises in Gerrard Street, Virginia came several times – a tall, alarming, infinitely distinguished looking figure with her thin beautiful face and deep-set eyes, her low-pitched but electrifying voice. Her clothes made a vaguer, dimmer accompaniment; they seemed to me to have been long, rather shapeless and in indefinite colours, acquiescent or subservient to her forceful personality.

In the summer of 1924 I wrote to a friend that 'the terrifying Virginia Woolf has asked me to dine. I feel she only wants to jeer at me but it would be cowardice not to go.' I was already much too fascinated by Bloomsbury *not* to go, and I did, but the next letter to the same friend was not very enthusiastic. St John Hutchinson had been the only other guest, had held forth a great deal; and Virginia had at length 'opened her mouth and delivered a slashing attack on the younger generation. As there was no one but myself present under forty, I felt rather uneasy. The chief cause for complaint was that they were too nice to their elders.'

She often launched these attacks on the young; I think they came from a sort of jealousy. Young writers or poets were particularly in danger, and those who were immune belonged to some very different world about which she could weave her marvellous fantasies – debutantes for instance, or Eddy Sackville-West, whom she urged to describe the complicated hierarchy of butlers and house-keepers at Knole. Probably one would have done just as well as a miner's daughter brought up in a council house.

Later, in 1926 I think, when Ralph Partridge and I were living in Gordon Square, we invited the 'Woolves' to din-ner. Alix Strachey, then in her thirties, and Julia Strachey came in afterwards. Virginia once more returned to the theme of the younger generation and gave an astonishing display of trying to charm them and make them look ridiculous at the same time. She certainly succeeded in the first.

Alix had (and has) a first-rate brain, but at this time was indulging in a post-dated passion for parties and dancing. Virginia greeted her with, 'Oh yes, Alix, I know all about you. You simply spend your whole time danc-ing, and sink further into imbecility every moment.' It was not really said as a joke, and led to a duel of wits be-tween Virginia and Alix. When they got on to psycho-analysis, Virginia was out of her depth, and worsted. (The Hogarth Press published translations of Freud, but I doubt if she had read much of them.) As they left, Leo-nard said to her. 'Come on, Virginia, don't disgrace the older generation!' To Julia Strachey, who was pretty and elegant, she had been entirely charming.

In the late twenties I sometimes went to Clive and Vanessa Bell's house, Charleston, for the week-end, and the 'Woolves' often came over from Rodmell for a meal. Sooner or later, gently coaxed by Clive, but not needing much to set her off, Virginia would launch into one of her dazzling performances – though that isn't the right word because they were entirely spontaneous. Argument was not her forte, but wild generalizations based on the flimsiest premises and embroidered with elaborate fantasy would be sent up like rockets, and thrive in the warm appreciation and laughter of her audience; and burgeon anew. Duncan Grant often interposed a comical remark and set her off again. Clive would roar with laughter (but she didn't seem to mind) and say, 'Ye – es, Virginia?' The pleasure of listening to what no one could mistake for anything but a manifestation of genius was so great that only the quality – none of the content – remains in my mind. There was no egotism about it. I'm sure she was enjoying herself, but so were we.

Sometimes we went over from Charleston to the 'Woolves' house. I remember one lovely summer afternoon in particular. We had all played bowls on the lawn, admired Leonard's gigantic flowers, and avoided his rather unappetizing dogs. I remember this occasion partly because Virginia chose me as her butt – she often liked to have one, like Alix formerly, and I saw her single out William Plomer once. She had a way of type-casting people, and if there had to be girls about she preferred them smart and frivolous. I had unfortunately been to Newnham and, worse still, Leonard had once said I had 'a logical mind'. So throughout the afternoon, as I remember it, she returned to the refrain 'but Frances has a logical mind', in the same vein as 'but Brutus is an honourable man' and with as deadly an effect. It was deadly, anyhow, to someone young, lacking in confidence and full of admiration; for I remember admiring the very barbs she stuck into me. Yet she showed that she wasn't really unkind – indeed I'm sure she had a layer of warm and sensitive kindness – by seeming suddenly to relent, turned all her magic on me, took me into the house, showing me the swallows' nest on top of the front door which prevented it ever being shut, and lending me a coat. I was completely bewitched.

The only other remark I remember from that afternoon was when she was talking about the mystery of 'missing' someone. When Leonard went away, she said, she didn't miss him *at all*. Then suddenly she caught sight of a pair of his empty shoes, which had kept the position and shape of his feet – and was ready to dissolve into tears instantly.

When she was carried away by her own talk Virginia often hugged herself in her folded arms and rocked her body from side to side.

This is all I can distil from my personal memories. Ralph had innumerable stories of the time he worked at the Hogarth Press. Though his period there ended in exasperation, as did that of most others, he always remained warmly devoted to them both. Stories of Leonard's obsessional meanness in no way detracted from this. Old envelopes were used and re-used, and every Christmas Ralph used to give Virginia a packet of Bronco, as a change from the cut-up pieces of galley proof or even brown paper which Leonard had hung in the lavatory.

There were stories, it must be admitted, of Virginia's extraordinary rudeness. How, when she was first introduced to Rosamond Lehmann (fatally young, beautiful, and a successful writer), who had not taken her latest manuscript to the Hogarth Press, she said bleakly: 'I really think, as Dadie Rylands is working for us and is such an old friend of yours, you might have brought your book to us,' and turned away. And to Molly MacCarthy (Desmond's wife): 'Molly you are dull. DULL, Molly, you are DULL, aren't you?' Whereas Molly was as far from dull as Virginia herself.

Janet Vaughan

(Adapted from an interview
in the BBC Television film
A Night's Darkness. A Day's Sail)

*I wonder if we can begin by talking about Virginia
Woolf's curiosity and the form it took. How did it affect
you personally?*

It affected me, I think, in two ways. First of all I believe
that one of the reasons why she liked seeing me and talking to me was because I was a scientist. I was an active
scientist, really doing things, and I could therefore give
her information. She had this passion for information
about practical things. For instance, when I started in my
very young days with all the mincing-machines that belonged to my friends and the odd pails that I borrowed
when making the first liver extract to be produced in
England – in a very Heath Robinson sort of way – I used
to talk to her about it and tell her what I was doing. She
found it fascinating; it was something quite outside the
world she had ordinarily met.

What sort of way did she ask you questions?

She would say, 'Just tell me, Janet, tell me what you do.'
It was the practical point of view that interested her. She
wanted to know how I borrowed the mincers and how
much liver I had. She wanted precise information, mark
you, she didn't want just fluff. And in the same way, I

think, she wanted precise information about people. If you were travelling with her or walking with her she would say, 'Look, there's that man wheeling his wheelbarrow, what do you think he had for breakfast?' She would be concerned about what he'd had for breakfast rather than what he had been doing – perhaps, what girl he'd been playing around with the night before. It was the practical things of people's lives which in an odd way intrigued her. I think she would sometimes ask what people thought, but basically she wanted facts about them.

Perhaps part of your happy relationship with her was based on the fact that you were related to her, and also that you were something of a rebel in your and her family. Could you tell us something about that?

Well, I was not a first cousin – I'm rather vague about cousins – but I was a cousin, and she had known in her childhood, or in her own time as a youngish woman, both my father and my mother. She had been very devoted to my mother, but didn't much care for my father. And I was a bit of a rebel; my father didn't approve of me and my ways.

Why not?

I don't really quite know. I think for one thing he didn't altogether approve of Virginia, and Vanessa and Clive Bell, and the way they ran their lives. He didn't therefore approve of the fact that I lived by choice in Bloomsbury as a medical student and as a young woman holding a job in a hospital. Also I was left wing in my political views. My father was a radical but he wasn't quite as left wing as I was. And so he firmly told my mother he had washed his hands of me. I think this was why Virginia so much disliked my father. She was devoted to my mother who was also a rebel. I think this was a link, so to speak, and also the fact that I was a woman who was doing a real job in the world. I never knew her as an ardent feminist; but I think she did like women to do things, and to do them with moderate success if possible. I had made a job for myself in the world and this was, to her, satisfying.

What was your impression of her in society – by which I don't mean at large parties but among friends?

She was a superb talker, and she generated talk with other people. For instance, if you could get her and Roger Fry arguing – the ball went backwards and forwards. She loved conversation. But I always thought she was much better and much happier with a few people. I saw her, I think, once at one of their plays which they did when there was a big party, but I always saw her with perhaps only a dozen people sitting out in the square in the evening, talking.

Who would some of those people be?

Well, the usual people: Clive Bell, Roger Fry, Leonard Woolf of course, Adrian Stephen, very rarely Lytton Strachey. I don't really remember seeing Lytton in the square.

Who was your favourite among them, apart from Virginia?

Frankie Birrell, who was of course a very great friend of my husband's. Frankie was one of the sweetest people in the world. And Julian Bell, who was Virginia's nephew. Julian was a very great friend of both my husband's and mine.

And Julian was perhaps particularly close to Virginia, would you say?

This I didn't realize. I knew that they were friends but I hadn't realized until quite recently that they were particularly close. He was a very lovable person of course, Julian.

Would you say that Virginia Woolf was a genius?

Well, what do you mean by genius? I would say it of very few people. I was discussing this question of genius the other day. It arose in connection with a scientist. I said of this scientist that I thought she had genius and this was what set her apart from other people working in the same field. I was talking to a physicist at the time and he said, 'What do you mean by genius?' I said, 'Well, it's a sixth sense. It's somebody who jumps a gap which other people would need a very, very solid bridge to walk across. I can't define it any better than that, but I think this is what Virginia did. She didn't do it as a scientist might, she did it by interpreting what she saw and what people might be thinking and how they interacted with one another. But she had this quality of jumping gaps, I think.

Can you recall any specific occasion when she manifested genius?

No, I don't think people do manifest it. You feel it. And judge it in their work – it comes out in people's work.

In which particularly of her works do you think it comes out?

Well, I think you'll find it in all the novels. Of course I

find *The Waves* very difficult, the earlier ones are much easier. But I think it's there in all of them – her capacity for observing and judging what people's reactions are with one another.

Would you tell me something about her appearance. How did it strike you?

She had enormous distinction and enormous beauty. It was a beauty of bone – it didn't matter whether she was young or old, it was irrelevant. And you do see this in rare people. Also I think it is a question of their intellect, of their minds shining through their faces. This scientist whom I was thinking of was very different from Virginia to look at, but she had this same extraordinary quality of beauty in her face, and distinction. For instance, if you met her in a train you would see it. You would feel at once, here is somebody quite out of the ordinary. I don't think that it's only beauty. The scientist I'm thinking of hadn't the same sort of beauty as Virginia, but it was the quality of mind coming through the face.

What was your impression of Leonard's relationship to Virginia?

Leonard was always there. He was there in the background, often saying very little, but you felt that he would pick up any bit that was dropped, and he would keep the peace if he could. Sometimes he would chip in with a fairly shrewd remark.

Did you feel that he was very protective towards her?

Very protective. But it was absolutely unostentatious, almost so that you didn't realize it. I think she was very much part of his life. I shall never forget seeing them one evening when he was leaving for a big Labour Party conference in the north and she was going with him as a party member's wife: she intended to do her job, not I think a public one, it was a job so to speak of a backroom girl. But it was very important to her and to him that this was just part of the pattern of their lives: that she might be the greatest novelist in one part of the world, but he was a very important person in the political sense and that she was involved in this too.

Did you ever stay in their house?

Yes, I stayed with them down in Sussex at Rodmell before I went off to America. It was the week-end before I went. It was typical of Virginia's quality that she asked me to stay the week-end before I left for a year in the States. I can't remember much what we did, we sat in their garden and we walked in the fields and we talked of course, because one always talked and talked with Virginia.

Angelica Garnett

ASKED to write about Virginia, the best approach seems to be through my mother Vanessa. These two Vs, angular and ambiguous, undecided whether to symbolize V or U. Both sisters started life with the same initials, V.S., then one changed to V.W., a variant on the original, the other to V.B., a round and solid addition. When I see V.B. on the registration plate of a car it immediately causes me a tremor of recognition. V.W. never seems to occur in such places.

Vanessa was the more practical, the more solid, the earthier of the two sisters. Virginia always said so, and the difference must have been marked even when they were young. Vanessa was the elder, a social success, married first and had children. She could mix colours, stretch canvases, cook meals and deal with unpalatable situations. She had a feminine capacity for listening tolerantly to the arguments and ideas of the men they both knew. This made a special place for her in the heart of Bloomsbury. Men from college, used to the freedom of masculine society or the polite and inconsequential chatter of their mothers and sisters, found it delightful to be listened to by a madonna with a sense of humour – a little wild perhaps and original, a little *sans façons* – how piquant it was and, in the end, how restful to be surrounded by a feminine atmosphere without the false obligations created by convention.

Virginia, on the contrary, was shy and awkward, often silent or, if in the mood to talk, would leap into fantasy and folly and terrify the innocent and unprepared. This combination of limpid beauty and demon's tongue proved fatal to those who were too timid to respond and who, ensnared while unconscious, woke like Bottom to find themselves in a fairyland echoing with malicious laughter.

Virginia remained always capable of demolishing the unwary: it was too easy for her, and it was a temptation that sometimes proved irresistible. Like many people who make inordinate demands, Virginia also had much to give; if she sometimes wounded her friends they forgave her and came back to her for her quality, the purity of which fascinated so many different people. It was like a diamond stream of water, hard and scintillating, transparent, bubbling, austere and life-giving.

When I knew her best, age and experience had softened her and lit her with a more tender light. She always looked vulnerable – those shadowy temples over which stretched a transparent skin showing threads of blue; the wrinkled waves of her high, narrow forehead; the taughtness of those sardonic lips pulled downwards at the corner; her bladed nose, like the breastbone of a bird or the wing of a bat, surmounted by deeply hooded melancholy grey-green eyes. She had the worn beauty of a hare's paw.

Like all the Stephens she was sad in repose – it seemed their most natural attitude – and yet the slightest ripple round her would cause a lightning-flicker in her eye, a flare of sympathy and intelligence. She was a great teaser and a shameless flatterer, avid for affection from those she loved. She adored nicknames: calling Vanessa Dolphin, herself Billy Goat or The Goat, I was Pixerina, Leonard was Leo – and so on. Virginia invented an extra personality for us, a luxury which we enjoyed but which half irritated, half amused, making us appear wonderfully changed as in a fairground mirror.

Virginia's version of Vanessa tended to soar into the Olympic regions, where she subconsciously felt that Nessa belonged. Like a highly coloured transparency held over the original design, sometimes it corresponded, sometimes not. She magnified the importance of Vanessa's practical abilities out of all relation to reality. It was true that Virginia could not bring herself to mend her clothes and preferred to pin up her silk rags with a gold brooch; but she could cook, and bottle fruit – well do I remember the pride she took in her cupboard of jade-green gooseberries and sad-purple raspberries on the stairs at Monks House. She also had a gift for appearances: the interiors of her houses were cool and civilized, the colours muted but various. There was in them nothing planned or self-conscious, though she was discriminating in her choice of objects and furniture. Leonard said that she saw things in antique shops from the window of the car which were nearly always worth stopping for.

Vanessa's strength lay in her closeness to reality, to the everyday world. By comparison she was calm, like a pool on which the coloured leaves slowly change their pattern. She accepted, rather than protested; was passive, rather than avid. She did not care deeply about abstract ideas, and was led by her sensibilities rather than her intellect. In theory she supported rationalism, though her own acts were usually compulsive. She instinctively limited her life to the two things she cared for most: her painting and her family. The wider world seemed to her to threaten these two points, and she appeared to choose the limits of her affection and sympathies. Love, with her, was an exclusive rather than an inclusive emotion; there was a chosen circle round which was planted a high palisade that cast its shadow both on those without and those within.

To Virginia, I think, Vanessa seemed at times formidable, embodying the spirit of justice and authority inherited from her Stephen ancestors. Virginia danced round her like the dragon-fly round the water-lily, darting in to attack and soaring away before Vanessa could take action. Vanessa had a kind of stoical warmth about her, a monolithic quality that reminded one now of the implacable smile of primitive Aphrodite, now of the hollow wind-whistling statues of Erewhon. She sat and sewed or painted or listened; she was always sitting, sometimes at the head of the table, sometimes by the fire, sometimes under the apple tree. Even if she said little, there emanated from her an enormous power, a pungency like the smell of crushed sage. She presided, wise yet diffident, affectionate and a little remote, full of unquenchable spirit. Her feelings were strong, and words seemed to her inadequate. She was content to leave them to her sister and to continue painting. Virginia's attitude was far from sitting, it was striding; long narrow thighs and shins in long tweed skirts, loping over the Downs, across the water-meadows, beside the river, or through the traffic in London, under the trees in the park and round the square. She was never placid, never quite at rest. Even when, knees angular under the lamp and cigarette in holder, she sat with a friend after tea, she quivered with interest in the doings of other people.

Leonard kept Virginia on very short purse-strings, allowing her so much pocket money a week. This she was free to spend as she chose, though she referred to her dependence in teasing, bantering terms. Since she had to count the shillings, she was more conscious of the pleasure they could bring. She adored shopping as much as any child and was ready to fall for the temptations of coloured string and sealing-wax, notebooks and pencils. We would visit Kettle's shop in New Oxford Street and supply ourselves with printed paper, glue and paper-clips, and sniff the curious smell of dust and brown paper. It was not unlike the smell of Virginia's writing-room in the basement of Tavistock Square, where she sat by the gas fire, surrounded by parcels of books and walls of paper. I did not go to see her there often. Usually I went upstairs, where we amused ourselves by making paper dolls and throwing lumps of sugar out of the window to the cart-horses. Enormously generous, Virginia (when she became richer) would pile presents on Vanessa and on me. As I grew older these took the form of clothes, and the afternoons spent in this way were less happy. The shop assistants made her feel shy and out of place, and she did not know how to say that a dress did not suit me or what to do about it, so we generally ended with some uneasy compromise relieved by the knowledge that we would soon be going home to tea and Chelsea buns.

The two families, Bells and Woolfs, met frequently. In London they saw each other on Sundays at Clive Bell's flat in Gordon Square; in the summer there were weekend tea parties held either at Monks House or at Charleston. There, if the weather was fine, tea was brought into the garden. Nessa presided at a very low table, while Virginia and Clive teased each other from the depths of Rorky chairs which squeaked when they moved. Clive was relaxed and reflective, puffing his pipe with pleasure, his clothes clean but old. Virginia often wore a hat, and

somehow combined elegance with angularity of movement. She seemed more subdued, more observant at
Charleston than at Monks House where she herself was
hostess. There we always had tea in the dining-room
which was sunk below the level of the garden, and dimly
green like a fish-pond. Indeed there was an aquarium in
one corner which I would stop to look at as Leonard's
shaking hands scattered ants' eggs for the fish to eat; they
would swim lazily to the surface to swallow, reject and
swallow again with apparent indifference. The plants on
the window-sills cast a green light into the room, and
through their interstices the legs and feet of late or unexpected visitors could be seen arriving. Here Virginia
waved her cigarette with infectious excitement and embarked on fantasies which made us hilarious. We egged
her on until Leonard punctured her sallies with a sardonic comment, or the flat statement that what she was
saying was completely untrue. Then we would troop into
the garden for the ritual game of bowls.

Apart from these family invasions the atmosphere of
Monks House was concentrated, quiet and mysterious.
Pen and ink replaced brushes and turpentine and there
were no manual occupations, except for Leonard's gardening. Often when one arrived he would emerge from
the bushes in shirt-sleeves, with clay on his boots and a
pair of secateurs in his hand. Then we would go together
in search of Virginia, to be found reading in or near her
garden-room under the chestnut trees by the churchyard.
Their chief amusement was conversation, and many different kinds of people came and went; the house was like
a sea-shell through which the water flows, leaving behind
it a taste of salt.

There were many occasions when I went to see Virginia alone with Vanessa, and I amused myself while

they enjoyed what they called a good old gossip. The intimacy of those occasions remains with me, and leads me to envy the relations between sisters. They understood each other perfectly and were probably at their best in each other's company. They were bound together by the past, and perhaps also by the feeling that they were opposite in temperament and that what one lacked she could find only in the other.

Rebecca West

I HAVE been asked for my recollections of Virginia Woolf. These are not many. We were no more than acquaintances. I met her not much more than twenty times, and I was never on terms of intimacy with her. I was not a member of her set. I find it difficult to make that statement without loading it with too many or too few implications. The Bloomsbury Group did not like me, and I did not like them. I should make two important exceptions to that rule. I found Clive Bell a gay and kind companion and Raymond Mortimer a pleasant and serious person. But the rest I found easy not to love, for reasons too complicated to state here. The situation was fascinating, if one put it into Proustian terms. Here was a group who resembled Madame Verdurin's clan but who thought they were the Guermantes; and what was fascinating was that they had all read Proust, they had seen their own situation analysed to the last trace element and did not recognize it. I recognize the same situation in the people of a younger generation who now celebrate the Bloomsbury Group; they too are Verdurins who think themselves Guermantes, and they too have read Proust.

It was so strange that in the centre of this prehensile group there was not a Madame Verdurin, but the Virginia Woolf, who would have found herself at home with few people in Proust except his grandmother. It is hard to describe her because she had a phantom-like quality. Though she sat opposite one, the impression left was as hard to recall as if she were one of those ghosts who are only seen as they turn the corner of a passage.

I have heard people say that they had gathered the two sisters were madonna-like. The Madonna is always represented as extremely tidy, even in the disadvantageous circumstance, such as the flight into Egypt. But Virginia and Vanessa were extremely untidy. They always looked as if they had been drawn through a hedge backwards before they went out. At the time I used to meet her I was untidy myself, being overworked and rather ill, but I always used to gain confidence from the sight of Virginia. There was a beautiful phrase, late Victorian and Edwardian, 'a well-turned-out woman'. Virginia was not well turned out. But she was certainly very beautiful in a Leonardo way. Both her face and her body could not have belonged to a person not of rare gifts. In the Crush Bar at Covent Garden I once heard a man say to his wife, 'Look at that funny-looking woman.' His wife peered through her glasses and objected, 'Ssh, you shouldn't say that about her, I'm sure she's . . .' and her voice died away in vague respect, almost awe. It was an authentic compliment.

She excited affection at once. The first time I ever met her was at a flat in Chelsea, in Royal Hospital Road, which was the home of two very remarkable women. One was the Editor of *Vogue*, Dorothy Todd, the other was the Fashion Editor, Madge Garland. Dorothy Todd was a fat little woman, full of energy, full of genius, I should say. Good editors are rarer than good writers, and she was a great editor, and Madge Garland was her equal. She was a slender and lovely young woman, who could have been a model had she not had all the equipment of a connoisseur of the first water. Together these women changed *Vogue* from just another fashion paper to being the best of fashion papers and a guide to the modern movement in the arts. They helped Roger Fry in firmly planting the Post-Impressionists in English soil and they brought us all the good news about Picasso and Matisse and Derain and Bonnard and Proust and Jean Cocteau and Raymond Radiguet and Louis Jouvet and Arletty and the gorgeous young Jean Marais. They also gave young writers a firmer foundation than they might have had by commissioning them to write articles on intelligent subjects at fair prices. There never was such a paper. Madge Garland is still with us. She was the first Professor of the art of Design at the Royal School of Art in South Kensington and she is today a font of wisdom about contemporary artistic achievement. What pleased me about Virginia Woolf was hearing her ask them questions about what they had seen and what they had done and whom they had met, with the happiest receptiveness.

They must have been of special use to her because of a disability she once confessed to me – and I think that her husband, Leonard Woolf, once wrote of it. She was no judge of writers of her own day. She edited a volume of letters written by various people to any correspondent they chose – real or imaginary – and I wrote 'A Letter to My Grandfather'. I sent it in too late for incorporation in the volume of the letters which the Hogarth Press published as there was illness in my family, but it was published separately as a pamphlet. Nobody has ever taken much interest in it except the critic Bonamy Dobrée, who liked it very much. After it had been published, a friend of mine met Virginia Woolf who said, 'Yes, we liked publishing Rebecca's letter but I did not understand this and that passage.' My friend was surprised, because he had understood it without difficulty and thought he must have been mistaken, but later, when I was dining with the Woolfs, I mentioned it to her and we got the pamphlet out and looked at it, and it really seemed very strange that she had not understood the passages she mentioned. Then she said to me, 'I don't believe you are being obscure in these passages, but I must own to a quality of mine which is a great defect in a critic. I don't really understand contemporary writers, and when I read them a sort of blindness comes over me.' I do not think she was merely being polite (though she was very polite) to cover up a fault of mine, for she afterwards asked me to write for the Hogarth Press. She wrote about James Joyce in an astonishing, almost stupid way. (Not that I am comparing my 'Letter to a Grandfather' with *Ulysses*.)

I remember a curious little drama, a period piece, in which this politeness of hers played a part. We all knew a Romanian diplomat called Antoine Bibesco, who had been brought up in Paris, and will be remembered by most people as a friend of Proust. He had married Asquith's daughter, Elizabeth, a very nice woman (who played a heroic part against the Nazis in Romania) and who wrote very novelettish little short stories, and when one volume of hers was published, Virginia Woolf either failed to review it or reviewed it unfortunately. This seemed quite extraordinary to both Antoine Bibesco and his wife and Antoine in genuine bewilderment found an occasion to discuss it with Virginia. They had a conversation which both parties afterwards related to me. Antoine told me that Virginia had betrayed to him the reason for her hostility. It was envy. She longed to lead a more glamorous social life than she did, to go to really great parties : as he put it, she wanted 'more chandeliers in her life'. But Virginia explained to me that Antoine had taken her by surprise and she had found herself telling him that Elizabeth belonged to such a gorgeous and superior world that she was unable to follow her when she described it in her novel. That Antoine should have misinterpreted this tactful explanation as a confession of disappointed social ambition was particularly funny considering that, though Virginia Woolf was very discontented with her work, and drafted and redrafted it times without number, she was beautifully contented with her niche in the world.

She instantly convinced my generation of her genius and I was also impressed by her originality. Because, of course, the attempts made to show that she derived from other writers – such as Dorothy Richardson – ignore chronology. The tendency to 'the stream of consciousness' technique was general, but she was as early as anyone in applying it. But I do not think her work merits the wholesale approval that is given it. *The Waves* is Pre-Raphaelite *kitsch* and should be forgotten. *A Room of One's Own* is on the right side and is a good piece of craftsmanship, but it is hardly worth while teaching it in schools, and indeed I think too much is made of *The Common Reader*. If you contrast her critical writings with those of her father, it is apparent what a much smaller world she inhabited. But there was this marvellous gift of perceptiveness, and the felicitous choice of what to perceive, which made her unique. For a few months we lived in a house near Rodmell, and it was a delight to see the wonderful garden which had been made by Leonard Woolf, who should have been a professional gardener. There among brilliant and profuse flowers that grew better for him than for anybody else, she sat and perceived them more blissfully than anybody else, I used to think it probable, in the world. She was a prodigy and one's heart still goes out to her. Yet I still do not understand everything about her. How could she have spoiled that exquisite book, *Orlando*, with those terrible photographs? How could she be so blind to some people? I once took to see the Woolfs, at Leonard's request, a woman from Kentucky who was staying with me. She was beautiful and elegant and witty and a remarkable historian, doing pioneer work in the history of the Indians of the South-West. Leonard was charmed by the visitor but I could see that Virginia was making nothing of her. I went back the next day to leave a book they wanted to borrow, and Virginia, sitting in an armchair, looked up at me and said, 'Leonard says your swan really was a swan. Describe her to me.' It was really the oddest mixture, this intense perceptiveness alternating with failure to perceive what was obvious to other people.

I am not conscious of her influence on the writers of today. It is odd how the French writers who think they are carrying on her method simply show that they do not read English very well. She did not catalogue, as the *nouvelle vague* does, she, I repeat it, perceived. It is an odd thing that the great writers of her time – Proust, Kafka, Joyce – had a horde of imitators immediately after their deaths, and then the flow ceased. She and they had carried their method so far that nobody could carry it any further.

There was something about her which was unusually clean, unsoiled. I never heard anybody relate a story about her which was tinged with anything that was not commendable. I remember having a foolish illusion when she died which shows this quality. Once she wrote me a delightful letter, and I had it framed and hung it on the wall of my room, with one from D. H. Lawrence on one side and one from George Moore on the other. Suddenly I looked up at the wall and Virginia's writing had disappeared. There was just an oblong of paper in the frame. Two days later I read in the paper that she was dead and for a dazed moment I thought idiotically, 'Ah, yes, she was politely trying to soften the shock, she was giving me a warning.' It is significant that an acquaintance, on pleasant terms but not a friend, should have so strong a feeling at her death.

William Plomer

BETWEEN the ages of fifteen and twenty-five I was out of England. I came back in 1929, and in the late spring of that year was invited to dine with Leonard and Virginia Woolf in Tavistock Square. I had never met them but they had been my publishers since 1925, when they had been encouraging about my first book.

I had sent the book to them because I liked what they had themselves written and published, and because their interest in literature was literary and not commercial. I had had correspondence with Leonard Woolf and knew that Virginia Woolf shared his interest in me as a writer. I dare say our meeting was preceded by mutual curiosity.

In those days a spring evening in Bloomsbury could be wonderfully peaceful. There was little or no traffic, and the leafiness of the gardens in the squares added to the peacefulness. I rang the bell and felt that I was probably the only dinner guest in Tavistock Square that evening. I was the only guest of the Woolfs, as it happened. The door was opened by Leonard Woolf, who gave me a searching look and a civil welcome, and led me up a couple of floors to where they lived. (The Hogarth Press functioned in the basement.)

I suppose I had a certain shyness, but they were so nice to me and I felt so easy with them that I really regarded them as friends from the moment we met. I had no preconceived ideas about Virginia Woolf's manner or presence. I knew she was a person of distinction but had no reason to suppose that she would be formidable, and the use of the word 'Bloomsbury' as a cultural or social definition was then almost unknown to me.

What I found, in the small drawing-room which owed some of its atmosphere to decorations and paintings by Vanessa Bell, and which seemed charming and secluded, was a woman of unique physical beauty and elegance. Her beauty was derived from the fineness of her features, her tall and slender figure, beautiful hands, and graceful movements. She had nothing whatever in common with popular or period or worldly beauties, or with any kind of conventional prettiness, and made an impression of combined strength and fragility – *nervous* strength and fragility.

Neither then nor at any other time did her clothes suggest either a concern with fashion or any effort to defy it. She knew, as people used to say, how to wear her clothes, which were neither simple nor complicated. She was not given to wearing ornaments, but what she was given to was smoking, after dinner, an excellent long cheroot. The cheroots came, I think, from the Army & Navy Stores, and she sometimes gave me a bundle of them to carry away.

The conversation was no doubt mostly questions from the Woolfs and answers from me. I was so different, I suppose, from their other authors and from the young Cambridge men of my generation whom they knew, that I must have been rather a problem to solve.

People have sometimes been surprised when I have said I thought Virginia Woolf a jokey person. She was in fact easily amused and we used to exchange what seemed to us entertaining anecdotes or gossip and to laugh a good deal. Occasionally one saw her convulsed with laughter, with tears in her eyes, and at such moments one became aware that she was being watched, perhaps with a touch of anxiety, by her husband. But one has only to glance at photographs of her to see that melancholy was not far away.

Leonard and Virginia Woolf were extremely kind to me. I was often asked to Tavistock Square (and later to Monks House for week-ends) and invited to meet their own friends, often people of rare distinction. It was at Tavistock Square, for example, that I first met T. S. Eliot, E. M. Forster, Lytton Strachey and Lady Ottoline Morrell (who once remarked to me that she thought Virginia Woolf's mouth the most beautiful she had ever seen). Virginia Woolf's affection for Eliot was evident. She and her husband had known him when he was unknown and had, I think, instantly perceived his quality as a man and a writer. There was something deferential to Virginia in his manner. She teased him a little, which was a good sign.

I was not then aware of, and did not perceive, the closeness of her past association with Strachey. In her conversation with Forster there seemed to be, on both sides, reservations. Lady Ottoline was admired by her for being a rebel against a stately, conventional, grand background and early environment, and for being, so to speak, on the side of culture.

At Monks House I learnt how devoted Virginia Woolf was to her sister, Vanessa Bell, and how fond of her nephews, Julian and Quentin Bell. And there one could perceive her constant alertness to literature and literary criticism, and the immense amount of work she did, not only as a novelist but as a literary essayist, to say nothing of her Diary and her letters. As a hostess she gave an impression of leisurely attention to her guests, and never of longing to get rid of them so that she could get back to her desk.

I didn't quite realize, until I read the printed extracts from her Diary, the extent of her doubts and anxieties about her novels, and her susceptibility to criticism of them; but I remember being surprised at her obvious pleasure when I rather diffidently told her how much I had been impressed by *The Waves* and that I liked it best among her novels. What I didn't tell her was that I have always preferred *The Common Reader* and its successors to her fiction.

*

I had when young some ability to tell character from handwriting. I had read books by graphologists but the faculty seemed largely intuitive. I was surprised sometimes by the amount of detail and the degree of accuracy in my diagnoses. Virginia Woolf was interested in my proceedings. 'Now, William,' she would say, 'I've got two or three handwritings for you to do,' and she would hand me envelopes addressed to her by persons not known to me.

With her curiosity as a novelist she obtained, through my guesswork, a new view of some of her acquaintances. Perhaps also the phrasing of my conclusions amused her, if only for the incidental light they threw on my own curiosity and social attitudes.

There was once an awkward moment when, addressed envelope in hand, I was in the middle of some uncomplimentary remarks about its writer, of whose identity I was unaware until it became clear that the person concerned was one of those present in the room. Was it not dangerously mischievous of V.W. to have made this situation possible? It made two of her guests uncomfortable and might have created for me a lifelong enemy.

I must say that I once caused her annoyance of rather the same kind. I was in a car with her and others returning to Monks House from some expedition and happened to be speaking of a certain marriage in the previous century. I said I thought it contemptible of the bride's parents to have objected to the bridegroom for reasons derived from class prejudice. In fact, I said, his family had been quite as estimable as hers.

I had not forgotten that in the front seat was a maid-servant who could hear our conversation. I thought the maid would hardly mind my having a dig at class prejudice, and in view of Leonard Woolf's socialism and his dislike of assumptions of social superiority I could hardly have annoyed him by what I was saying. But Virginia Woolf palpably winced, and I feared she must have thought that I had failed to show consideration for the maid's feelings. Later in the afternoon, telling somebody where we had been and what we had done, she alluded to what I had said, and in her tone there was a perceptible asperity. If I had been clumsy, I deserved it; if not, not. In either case this was the only occasion on which she was ever anything but perfectly amiable in her manner towards me.

*

I have heard people suggest that she could be 'cruel', but have no knowledge of this. And 'Wasn't she rather frightening?' I have been asked. I can't say I was ever frightened of her, though I wouldn't single her out as a woman with an exceptional power for putting everybody at their ease and keeping them there. Confronted with her quick intelligence and acute sensibility, one might have had to exert one's own blunter faculties, and for some this exercise could have provoked a sense of strain, mingled with alarm.

Leonard Woolf once remarked to me, after her death, that she could be 'censorious', but, he said, 'That wasn't the real Virginia.' A person more sensitive than most may be more liable to be critical of insensitiveness, and how can anybody with high critical standards fail to censure what seems trashy, trite, false or pretentious? Better censoriousness than a sloppy tolerance.

When the novels of Charles Morgan were being a good deal read and often written or spoken about solemnly, she looked into one and was so exasperated by it that she threw it out of a window. Whatever the effect of fiction upon readers, its defenestration cannot be recommended. Bodily harm might be caused to passers-by, and although reviewers sometimes say they have been bowled over by a book, who would wish to be *literally* bowled over by a novel?

Why did the book irritate her? Clearly because there was something in Morgan's attitude to life and character – something solemn, perhaps, portentous, romantic, high falutin' – so utterly different to her own that she found it intolerable.

*

There were persons whom Virginia Woolf used to tease, not unkindly. One hardly bothers to tease people unless one likes them. I don't think Leonard Woolf at all cared for Hugh Walpole, whom I met at Tavistock Square, and at whom he tended to glance sideways with the look of a restive horse, but Virginia liked him, and liked teasing him.

Walpole was often sneered at, in print and in talk, and his ebullience did make him an easy target, but in fact he had a real respect for creative artists and their works, and an enthusiasm for evidence of talent in writing and painting. This led him to admire and respect Virginia Woolf and to delight in whatever attention she paid him. They were as different as they looked: he was portly, pink and fussy; she was slender, elegant and controlled. She seemed astonished and amused by his fluency and large public as a writer; he respected her prestige.

It was part of Walpole's character, or destiny, as can be seen in Sir Rupert Hart-Davis's life of him, to find himself in slightly absurd situations, and his pleasure in going to Buckingham Palace in a top hat to be knighted seemed to her absurd. When Walpole told her proudly that he had been offered and had accepted a knighthood, she had said, 'Oh, Hugh, how *could* you?'

*

I don't know if either Virginia or Leonard Woolf was ever offered any decoration. If she had lived longer, such an offer must surely have been made. Either would, I feel sure, have declined, believing that the only honours of value to a creative artist or a thinker are those of having done his or her best and of being respected by those, living or dead, most fitted to understand and enjoy what he or she has done.

It is arguable that it shows an excess of self-esteem, a kind of arrogance, an assumption of superiority, to regard oneself as being above accepting tokens of public recognition. 'Diogenes,' wrote Sir Thomas Browne, 'I hold to be the most vainglorious man of his time, and more ambitious in refusing all Honours, than Alexander in rejecting none.'

This brings us to the assumption, sometimes made by reviewers and other literary journalists, that what they call 'the Bloomsbury Group', and Virginia Woolf as one of its so-called 'members', gave themselves airs of superiority. I don't think they were affected: what they had was a kind of self-confidence or self-assurance which could be irritating to persons so unsure of themselves that they were apprehensive of being snubbed or, worse still, ignored.

One could call this self-assurance a class thing and a period thing. Virginia Woolf and her Bloomsbury friends were Victorians by birth, and came from a highly educated, property-owning and professional stratum of society; and her father, Leslie Stephen, was a mandarin, if ever there was one. With such a background, one is liable to treat one's judgement in social, intellectual and aesthetic matters a shade too confidently – or at least to appear to do so. Certainly some of the Bloomsburys – Lytton Strachey, for instance – could be completely unforthcoming and could appear supercilious when introduced to strangers. Lord David Cecil has remarked that when one first met them they would offer their hands but nothing like a smile of greeting.

If, like her friends, Virginia Woolf could seem armoured with a kind of intellectual arrogance, I can't say I noticed it myself. She never made me feel that she felt indifferent or cold towards me. And did not her curiosity save her from aloofness? Her life was one long inquiry into the nature of personality and of what one may as well call reality or truth. And surely a nature more given to asking than to dogmatizing is chiefly 'superior' in its refusal to take for granted what other people do take for granted.

I never noticed anything haughty or snubbing in her

manner towards others – teasing, yes; ironical, yes; inquisitive, yes. Sometimes her curiosity about people would lead her to ask them a succession of questions, and even while they were in the course of answering she would begin to invent a little myth about them, and make teasing, fanciful statements about their motives and doings which they would quickly deny or modify.

*

When Julian Jebb made a film about Virginia Woolf, several of the contributors said unhesitatingly that she was a genius. Is such a label important? Does it add to her quality as a writer to call her a genius?

An obsessive concern with writing or any other art is not in itself evidence of genius, but persons of genius do have such a concern. Virginia Woolf had a more than ordinary singlemindedness: everything seemed to contribute to her interpretation of life. And if a genius is somebody who brings something new I think one could say that she had something very like genius.

She has been and still is very much read, I suppose more by women than men, and her view of life as a sort of animated mosaic, with a lot of things impinging on the senses or going on at different levels at the same time, has probably had an influence, which is difficult to estimate, on the way many people look at life, as well as an influence on the way they write about it. I can't help thinking that in France, where she has, I suppose, been much read, she has influenced the novelists of the *nouvelle vague* – Alain Robbe-Grillet, Claude Simon and others – with the broken time-sequence, the interior monologue, a sense of the importance of inanimate objects, with the evocation of momentary atmospheres, and with resurgences of memory. Looking back, I revere her honesty.

One must not call a Hugh Walpole or a Charles Morgan dishonest. They were successful entertainers of many readers in their day, but their fantasies do not seem to wear as well as the truth-seeking of Virginia Woolf.

*

(Written in 1941, the year of Virginia Woolf's death)

Once when Virginia Woolf was sitting beside Lady Ottoline Morrell on a sofa their two profiles were suddenly to be seen, one in relief against the other, like two profiles on a Renaissance medal or coin – two strange queens who had come from the leisured, ceremonious nineteenth century, each, by being herself, to win an allegiance to herself in the twentieth. Both faces were aristocratic, but in that chance propinquity it was startling how much more finely bred, or shall we say delicate, Virginia's face appeared. The two women admired and were affectionate towards one another. They had a good deal in common. Both had what old-fashioned people call presence – great dignity and style, yet great simplicity. Ottoline Morrell, though not always discriminating about people, certainly understood the uniqueness of Virginia. Virginia spoke admiringly of the intelligence and force of character which had enabled Ottoline to emerge from the grand but narrow world into which she was born (and of which she retained the grandeur) into a more varied world in which ideas and talent counted more than property or background.

Both had an insatiable curiosity about their fellow-creatures, and both the love of gossip (in no disparaging sense of the word) and the capacity to be amused or astonished which goes with that virtue. In the exercise of this curiosity the difference in their approach was as striking as the difference in their profiles. Ottoline would ask the most personal leading questions, not in a hectoring way, but without the slightest compunction, and with the manner of a feudal grandee who had a right to be told what she wanted to know. (Since most people like talking about themselves to a sympathetic listener she often got what she wanted.) Virginia's approach was less blunt and more ingenious. With a delicious and playful inventiveness she would often improvise an ironical fantasy about the life and habits of the person to whom she was talking, and this was likely to call forth protests, denials and explanations which helped to make up a confession. Ottoline, less vulnerable and less discerning, could get on with Tom, Dick and Harry, while Virginia sometimes frightened people by aloofness or asperity, for which they had only their own clumsiness to blame; but in the course of several hours in the company of an individual who, she afterwards admitted, caused her alternate emotions of anger, laughter and utter boredom, she showed no sign of the first two and only a faint trace of the last – which is in any case the most difficult of the three to hide.

The fact that she did not make, either in social life or in her books, any concession to vulgarians, or offer any foothold to a banal understanding, or bait any traps for popularity, probably helped to create a legend about herself among the uninformed which still exists – a legend of a precious, fragile and superior highbrow shut up in an ivory tower in Bloomsbury and completely out of touch with 'ordinary' or 'normal' people (whoever they may be). The legend is quite false and hardly worth refuting: in any case Bloomsbury, as a term of abuse, had its origin in envy and ignorance, was almost meaningless, and is by now trite and pointless. If Virginia lived in an ivory tower, it consisted mostly of windows and was very hospitable, and she was as often out as in. Her life was rich in experience of people and places, and her disposition, as is sometimes the case with those who are highly strung and have an inclination to melancholy, was genial. A biographer, so far from having to chronicle the life of a recluse, might be embarrassed by the richness of his material. Think, for instance, of Virginia as a young girl, anything but assured, going in a cab to a ball at a great house, wearing a modest string of pearls ('but they were real pearls'); Virginia learning Greek with Clara Pater, the sister of Walter, in Canning Place, in a setting of blue china, Persian cats, and Morris wallpapers; the Dreadnought Hoax, one of the world's great practical jokes; Virginia bathing with the slightly bow-legged Rupert Brooke; Virginia sitting up all night in a Balkan hotel reading the *Christian Science Monitor* to cheat the bugs; the murder under her window in Euboea; Virginia continuing to play bowls at Rodmell during the Battle of Britain, with Spitfires and Messerschmitts fighting, swooping and crashing round her.

In each of us there are two beings, one solitary and one social, but no more separate than a man from his shadow, which goes with him everywhere, sometimes throws him into relief, disappears altogether in twilight, darkness or an even radiance, and grows immensely long towards sunset. There are people who cannot bear to be with others, and turn into hermits or something worse; most cannot bear to be alone, and so become common and shallow. In Virginia the two beings had an equal life and so made her a complete person. She could be detached and see things in perspective; and she could enter into things, into other people's lives, until she became part of them. The two beings can be perceived in her writings, sometimes distinct, sometimes merged. The special genius of her rare and solitary spirit reached its purest expression in *The Waves*, an exquisite, subjective book nearer to poetry and music than the novel. The social being in Virginia, the novelist, can be seen most essentially not in her fiction but in *The Common Reader*. Those essays are full of warmth, shrewdness, knowledge of the world and of human nature, qualities which, though discernible in her novels, are less important there than her own sensitivity, as an instrument, to the vibrations of the external world.

The old masters of fiction (Shakespeare, Balzac, Tolstoy) are such because, in addition to all the other necessary gifts, they are tough guys and men of the world with an exceptional robustness and gusto; they have also an extreme preoccupation with sociology. This preoccupation, when it goes more with finesse than with animal spirits, produces novelists like Jane Austen, Flaubert or Proust, and it was to such writers that Virginia Woolf was in some ways akin. It might be argued that her myth-making faculty was chiefly applied to sensations rather than to characters, and that her passion for sociology was in a sense scientific. Although she enjoyed embroidering facts about people in a poetic or ironical way, she was really devoted to the facts themselves. The solitary being was a poet, the social being was a sort of scientist. The former discovered poetic truth, the latter anthropological truth. During the last ten years of her life Virginia said over and over again how much more she enjoyed reading autobiographies than novels. She was heard to say that almost any autobiography was more satisfying than a novel. When autobiographies were written by people she knew and who were congenial to her – Lady Oxford, for instance, and the bluff and breezy Dame Ethel Smyth – she not only had the pleasure of getting to know them better, but her appetite for social knowledge and reminiscence was very much gratified. A passionate precision in collecting data about society (very strong in Flaubert and Proust) made her delight in anything that helped it. Thus, when a friend of Virginia's revealed a faculty for telling character from handwriting, she was much pleased and amused by his revelations, which, though not infallible, were occasionally penetrating. And sometimes she would make the joyful discovery that A most unexpectedly knew B. How? Why? Where? What was the link between them?

The artist is engaged in a constant effort to create order out of the haphazard, singleness out of multiplicity, to trace a pattern that can be seen in the universal pattern of life, which is too vast and various to comprehend. Virginia's extraordinary consciousness of the complexity of things and her ability to come to terms with that complexity made her value people who could do likewise, and if there was one thing more than another which her friends had in common it was their power of being articulate, like herself, in a new way. It was therefore not surprising to see her, at one time and another in that upper room in Tavistock Square, happy in the company of, for example, Lytton Strachey, Lowes Dickinson, Roger Fry, E. M. Forster, T. S. Eliot, Stephen Spender, Elizabeth Bowen or Rosamond Lehmann. She had a great gift for making the young and obscure feel that they were of value too; she admired physical as well as intellectual beauty; she could charm away diffidence; and she could be notably sympathetic with young women, particularly young women from Cambridge. A strong sense of the proper functions of literature and the importance of taste gave her a proper pride (derived doubtless in part from her literary father and background) in her own gifts, but she was absolutely without arrogance, and no beautiful woman ever wore her beauty more modestly. Though her nervous vitality was much greater than her bodily strength, Virginia was a hard worker, not only at reading and writing, but as a publisher and at times a printer, with her husband. She read a vast number of MSS for the Hogarth Press, books which rightly bore the imprint of 'Leonard and Virginia Woolf'. No writer, known or unknown, could have wished for a more imaginative and percipient publisher's reader, or one with more openness to new ideas. She was generous in her encouragement of younger writers, and was never, like those old fogeys, who have lately been 'hunting the high-brow' in *The Times*, impeded by middle-aged prejudices. Indeed, one never thought of her in terms of age, but only of quality. This rare creature, simply by being herself, had won an international reputation, and in the Far East, as well as in Europe and America, she has evoked a response in the responsive. Those who have known Leonard and Virginia Woolf have known civilization, and one person at least has often, seeing them together, been reminded of that line of Crabbe's about happy marriages: 'They are not frequent, but they may be found.'

To write a few memorial pages about Virginia is an honour, a grief, and a pleasure: a pleasure, because it has always been and must always be pleasing to think of her. To write about her briefly is to be inadequate: she was many-sided, and many would have to write about her to bring her to life at all on paper. She loved the great abstractions, like truth and justice; she loved London and the country, her relations and friends; she loved her domestic surroundings; she loved the written word. She liked good talk, good food (and plenty of salt with it) and good coffee. I see her in a shady hat and summer sleeves,

moving between the fig tree and the zinnias at Rodmell;
I see her sitting over a fire and smoking one of her favourite cheroots; I see the nervous shoulders, the creative
wrists, the unprecedented sculpture of the temples and
eye-sockets; I see her grave and stately, or in a paroxysm
of happy laughter, and I shall never see her again.

David Garnett

I HAD met Virginia Woolf at intervals since I had first got to know her brother Adrian in 1910, but it was not until I was living at Charleston that I got to know more than that she was a very beautiful woman, tall, with large green eyes, a lovely forehead and aquiline features, who flashed in and out of our company and was on the most intimate terms with Vanessa. Both sisters might have been models for the sculptors who made the doorways of Chartres Cathedral. But though they were very much alike, their beauty contrasted. Vanessa was the Virgin, with Quentin an infant Jesus in her arms; Virginia a saint or angel, with none of the beauty of maternity. In company there was as much contrast in their behaviour as in their looks. For whereas Vanessa was reserved and domestic, disliking going outside the circle of her intimate friends, Virginia was a woman of the world who enjoyed making excursions into society and bringing back stories of her encounters.

Perhaps the greatest difference between the sisters was in their voices and manner of speaking. Vanessa's voice was clear and even. She spoke, particularly when she was giving her opinions, as though she was reading aloud in accents of balanced beauty the sentence of the court. Only when she was provoked by an interruption would she flash back, but even then her voice was quiet and controlled. Virginia, holding a cigarette, would lean forward before speaking and clear her throat with a motion like that of a noble bird of prey, then, as she spoke, excitement would suddenly come as she visualized what she was saying and her voice would crack, like a schoolboy's, on a higher note. And in that cracked high note one felt all her humour and delight in life. Then she would throw herself back in her chair with a hoot of laughter, intensely amused by her own words.

Vanessa lived in a closed room; when Virginia came over from Asheham she brought the wind off the Downs into the house with her. She had a warmth and goodfellowship which set people at their ease; she had the gift for sudden intimacy which I had found so charming in D. H. Lawrence when I had first met him. Her voice and her glance were filled with affection, mockery, curiosity, comradeship. She would put a hand on one's shoulder and as she propelled one about the garden, between flowerbeds, she would ask some reckless question which flattered and disturbed. Her interest was exciting and left one tingling with satisfied vanity or doubts about oneself.

She was particularly interested in young people and children, so that her visits from Asheham were a signal for rejoicing on the part of Julian and Quentin who had secrets to share with her. Thus she was always led aside and from the corner of the walled garden where they were ensconced came her clear hoot of laughter – like the mellow hoot of an owl – and Julian's loud explosions of merriment, protests and explanations.

Virginia was a wonderful raconteur – she saw everyone, herself included, with detachment, and life itself as a vast Shakespearean comedy. She loved telling tales at her own expense – some of them as ribald as anything in Chaucer – for all her personal vanity was forgotten in the storyteller's art. But alas, while I was living at Charleston I almost deliberately avoided having a friendship with Virginia, for it would have been impossible without confidences and in the home circle she had the reputation of a mischief-maker. We were all on edge enough owing to the war without running any unnecessary risk of letting Virginia embroil us with each other. Thus it was only later on that I became on terms of close friendship with Virginia and then our friendship grew steadily, until, when my hair was streaked with grey, I became not Bunny, but her dear Badger. By then she had for me long ceased to be a possible mischief-maker and became the very opposite – a woman on whose sympathy and understanding I could rely when I most needed support.

Her work always interested and excited me. She is one of the very few writers I have known who was never satisfied to repeat herself but was always experimenting and developing and in that respect I have tried to follow her example. There was much of the same reckless imagery in her conversation that gives such individuality to her novels. Such things as her description in *Jacob's Room* of Southampton Row:

Chiefly remarkable nowadays for the fact that you will always find a man there trying to sell a tortoise to a tailor. 'Showing off the tweed, sir; what the gentry wants is something singular to catch the eye, sir – and clean in their habits, sir!' So they display their tortoises...

Virginia wrote *A Haunted House* in the collection of experimental sketches and impressions which she published in *Monday or Tuesday*, and that lovely sketch evokes the ghost of Asheham, a house with a personal character as individual as that of a woman one has loved, and who is dead. For many years Asheham House has only been a ghost, for though it is standing its surroundings have been utterly transformed. An immense heap of spoilage has been dumped into the flat meadow in front of it, entirely shutting out the view. This is now overgrown with briars and bushes and young trees. Huge sheds, warehouses and a roasting oven with a tall chimney fill the old farmyard. . . To visit Asheham House today is a rude lesson in the importance of economics.

Places explain people. They become impregnated with the spirit of those who have lived and been happy in them. For a full understanding of Virginia, who spent her holidays and week-ends there for several years after her marriage, Asheham would greatly help. But the clue has almost gone – it is more a memory than a reality and in common with all the houses which Virginia made her own there was a suggestion in it of a timeless, underwater world.

Alix Strachey

(Mrs James Strachey)

I DID not know Virginia Woolf well. We were not close personal friends, but I met her many times. She was so much part of the Bloomsbury scene when I was living in Bloomsbury – indeed, one felt she was the centre of it – that hardly a day went by in which I did not meet her, or hear her talked about by my friends and by almost everyone I met.

I saw her first of all at one of Ka Cox's parties. At this time, 1916, I was sharing a flat with my brother, Philip, near Mecklenburgh Square in Bloomsbury. We had both just come down from Cambridge. Ka had rooms in one of the Inns, I think it was Lincoln's Inn, and Philip took me to one of her evenings. Ka was a great hostess; she had many friends and by mixing them all together at her parties she helped to bridge the gap between the extremely highbrow Bloomsbury Group and the other perhaps more friendly people whom I knew.

I enjoyed myself enormously on this particular evening. It was the first time since moving to London that I had come across liberal conversation on all sorts of subjects. I met James Strachey, whom I came to know well and whom a few years later, I married. I also met Carrington again then an ex-Slade School student and an old friend of mine James and Carrington already knew Virginia well and it was through them, at Ka's party, that I first met and talked to her.

Virginia had then just recovered from a serious mental breakdown. I had been told that she had put on a lot of weight owing to the effects of her illness and to the medical treatment she had received afterwards. I was surprised to hear this, as I found it difficult to picture her as anything other than thin. When I saw her at Ka's she was still a little plump but had already begun to lose weight. Perhaps the plumpness became her, because she was what I can only call absolutely exquisite.

She was like somebody belonging to another world and I was entranced by her. She had huge eyes which at the same time seemed hollow, almost as though set deep in a cavern. Her nose was aquiline, her eyebrows delicate and arched. They gave the impression that she was surprised at what she saw going on around her – in fact, at being there at all. She had a lovely musical voice, but even this did not alter the effect of not quite belonging to the world.

Some of her friends say that she moved rather clumsily, but I never had this impression. I would say that she was particularly graceful. Not in a worldly sense, because she did not have the manner of someone used to worldly society, but she moved easily and quickly. She seemed tall, probably taller than she was, because her clothes were long and elegant. They had the appearance of draperies and especially suited her; they made her seem to float as she walked. This floating, ethereal effect, however, did not apply to Virginia's nature. She was not angelic in any way, in fact quite the opposite. I thought that she had a rather mocking spirit.

Her laugh could be a little malicious too, but unlike other members of the Bloomsbury Group she was malicious not behind one's back but to one's face. She made fun of people in public and used to weave ideas about them. They were fantasies which she knew to be fantasies. For instance, she would say to me, 'Now Alix, I wonder what you are really like. I think you must be rather like a bat because I am sure you have a night life.'

There was another fantasy which she enjoyed elaborating, it made me feel rather uncomfortable but it was amusing and, I suppose, true in a way. She thought that I was not only a bat but a badger as well. Her reason for this, she said, was that when I got hold of an argument I never let go. I am not sure what the habits of badgers are, but I think she meant that if I made a point during a conversation and it was not answered in the way I expected it to be, then I became a badger. Her remark was true in that I found an argument interesting and did not like people wandering from the point.

Sometimes she said things that made people very angry, but nobody contradicted her vehemently. We felt that somehow she was too vulnerable, too easily injured mentally to lose one's temper with. For my part, I felt that anything I might say in reply would be clumsy compared to her choice of words and, in any case, she never made me angry enough to want to try. It always seemed strange to me that the sensibility which was evident in all her writing was not really present in her daily life. People were not quite real to her and if her fancy ran away with her she might say almost anything.

Lytton Strachey could be rather malicious too, but there was a difference in that he was always aware of the person he was talking to. His rudeness was deliberate and his choice of words was calculated to annoy. With Virginia it was not so. To her, people were rather like cardboard figures; she did not expect them to mind at all. I know that Virginia showed great interest and curiosity about the character and doings of other people, but it seemed to me that her wish to know all about them sprang ultimately from a feeling of alienation from reality – an alienation which she was trying to overcome.

But this was only one aspect of Virginia's character. She really had a great sense of humour and there was usually an air of immense gaiety about her. Lytton, in particular, could bring out these qualities in her. They had a great deal of badinage together and it was always amusing to hear them. I think it was prompted by the fact that they were a little frightened of each other. It was not quite the same as being jealous, because they respected each other's work, but Lytton may have felt that Virginia's art was in a sense more spiritual, more elevated in some ways than his.

Lytton is to me so readable that I find it hard to realize he is now classified as being a first-class writer. If ever I have nothing to do I pick up a book by him and become entertained at once. He had the sort of imagination that I can follow easily. He may have felt, because he was so readable, that he was a little more ordinary compared to Virginia and that she was more sublimated. It was something like that. I cannot be certain about Virginia's point of view either, I did not know her well enough, but Lytton's books were a great success and she may have felt put out to some extent by this. In any case, whatever the cause, the badinage between them was always amusing and one knew that underlying it all there was a deep mutual affection.

Whenever I saw Leonard and Virginia together I noticed how marvellous he was with her. He completely arranged his life and hers so that she would have the minimum of mental strain. I think she needed someone as firmly anchored mentally as he was and I am sure that he was the only person who could have kept her going. At a party or among a group of friends he would provide the backbone of the conversation and then be happy to let her ornament it if she wanted to.

Leonard was much more straightforward to talk to, but I think that he could be rather severe at times. Not with Virginia, of course, but in his manner with other people. One felt that he never liked being contradicted very much, and if one tried to put a personal view to him other than his own then he would look rather grim and not answer. Virginia used to tease him a little on these occasions, but he always let her do or say anything she liked as long as he thought it would not damage her peace of mind.

I had the impression that Virginia's sister, Vanessa, was very important to her too. I saw them both from time to time in London and at Asheham or Charleston. I noticed that she always looked to Vanessa for a feeling of security, even during her married life. Vanessa was very different from Virginia, she was much more placid. She was beautiful too, but not in so ethereal a way; her nose was shorter and her face more oval. These differences made her good looks more classical.

Leonard and Virginia loved the peace of the Sussex countryside. They very often took their friends to stay with them at Asheham, the small country house they had rented near Lewes. When they were there Leonard encouraged her to do a certain amount of domestic work, such as cooking. He thought it was good for her to relax from the strain of writing. He rather laid out, wherever they were, what her working hours should be and her hours of recreation. Asheham was a particularly lovely house in which to relax at week-ends. It had a dreamy quality about it, almost haunting. It was much more enchanting, I thought, than Monks House which they eventually moved to in Rodmell.

Near the end of the war, I think it was in 1917, Leonard and Virginia asked me if I would like to work at the Hogarth Press. It was to set up type for their second publication, *Prelude*. I had just finished reading French and English literature at Newnham and did not know exactly what type of work I wanted to take up. I had no intention of writing literary books at all, but I accepted their offer because I thought it would be an introduction to literary work of some sort.

On my first day at the Hogarth Press I sat on a high chair in a top room and was shown, by Leonard and Virginia, how to do the setting up. I had to pick out tiny pieces of type with forceps and place them face up into a metal frame. After I had slowly and painstakingly grasped the idea they said, 'Well, we'll leave you to it now', and then, to my surprise, they went out for a walk. I did the setting up for some hours until an awful boredom came over me. I began to think that it was no introduction to literary work, it was more like a dead end to any career. I knew that I would never be interested enough to do the type-setting quickly or well. When they came back I told them, to their astonishment, that I could not possibly carry on, it was much too boring. As far as I can remember, my introduction to a literary life lasted no longer than one day.

This incident did not make any difference to our friendship. I saw them again many times, particularly when James and I moved into Gordon Square. We had taken a large house so that we could share it with many of our friends. None of us had much money in those days and we tended to herd together. Lytton, Carrington and Ralph Partridge had rooms there at various times; Lydia

Lopokova, before her marriage to Maynard Keynes, was living in a flat on the ground floor. Leonard and Virginia came to see our friends as well as to see us.

In 1920 James and I went to live in Vienna. This meant that all the interests we shared with the people we knew in Bloomsbury changed in a way that affected us considerably. James was studying psychology in Vienna as one of Freud's pupils. I studied with him and afterwards we stayed on to translate some of Freud's clinical papers. Our new friends and acquaintances were nearly all analysts. They were not essentially interested in art or literature and I began to feel cut off from our Bloomsbury associations.

When we finally returned to England, the situation was still the same. James deplored the change, too. He was sure that Lytton felt we had entered a world so different from his own that he would never be able to share it with us. Our new world, governed as it was by a knowledge of the unconscious mind, was alien not only to Lytton; it frightened a lot of people and some of them were a little contemptuous of it.

Even Leonard seemed to be on the defensive. I remember one instance which occurred quite recently. He had made a speech to a number of analysts at an anniversary the Hogarth Press was celebrating and, afterwards, was talking to me about emotions – or, more precisely, the lack of them. He said there was one emotion which he never felt – I forget which particular one it was now – and I said to him casually, 'How do you know you don't in your unconscious mind?' I thought we would have an interesting discussion about it, but instead he looked rather hurt and moved away.

James often wondered why Leonard did not persuade Virginia to see a psychoanalyst about her mental breakdowns. There were analysts with sufficient knowledge to understand her illness in those days. Although this knowledge was available, I did not agree with James that it would be of help to Virginia. Leonard, I think, might well have considered the proposition and decided not to let her be psychoanalysed. Her form of illness was probably what is called manic-depressive; analysis can improve some people suffering from this, but it is not always a certain method. It is possible that something in her mind might have become too strongly stirred up and she would have been made worse. Certain types of patient – for instance, common or garden hysterics – often become wrought up to a considerable degree at some stage in their analysis, and I think that with Virginia's very parlous mental balance it might have been too much for her. Today, of course, now that so much is known about drugs, she would receive very different treatment. At that time, sedatives were mainly used, and I think that if you give enough sedatives to be effective then there comes a point at which the patient ceases to exist as an individual.

Virginia's imagination, apart from her artistic creativeness, was so interwoven with her fantasies – and indeed with her madness – that if you had stopped the madness you might have stopped the creativeness too. It seemed to me quite a reasonable judgement for Leonard to have made then, if he did so. It may be preferable to be mad and be creative than to be treated by analysis and become ordinary.

Virginia's breakdowns were brought on partly by exhaustion after finishing a novel, but very largely by the fact that she had intensified her fantasies while writing it, to such an extent that they had probably become uncontrollable. It is likely that this tendency was born in her and, the more she concentrated on her work, the more exaggerated it became.

Virginia was absolutely devoted to Leonard and realized that he had given up a lot for her – perhaps not given up, but he had always arranged his life for her benefit. In 1941, after finishing her last novel, Virginia felt that she was 'going mad again'. These were her own words. She did not want to go on living because she was sure that she was ruining Leonard's life and so broke away, as it were, from his devoted protection and killed herself.

Virginia did not talk about her breakdowns to us; we only knew through Leonard's continuous care of her that from time to time she needed rest. Also, she very seldom mentioned her work. But there is one discussion I had with her which I particularly remember. We were comparing poetry with prose. She said that the goodness in prose was a higher goodness than that in poetry. She maintained that prose had its own rhythm, much more subtle, much less evident and quite different from poetic rhythm. She meant, of course, the poetry of her day in which the rhythm was more obvious. I was very much impressed by this. Whether she was only playing with an idea, I am not sure, because she loved starting such ideas.

I have always found Virginia's flights of imagination in her work difficult to follow. Mine do not go along the same lines as hers, but this does not stop me from admiring them. I can see her imagination 'leave the ground', as Leonard has said, and I can marvel at it, but I cannot really enjoy it. I think that what she wrote was very beautiful – to use an old-fashioned word – but it is as though I am too earthbound to be able to appreciate it fully. In spite of this, it is not possible to think of Virginia as an ordinary writer whom one might or might not like. She was always obviously something very special.

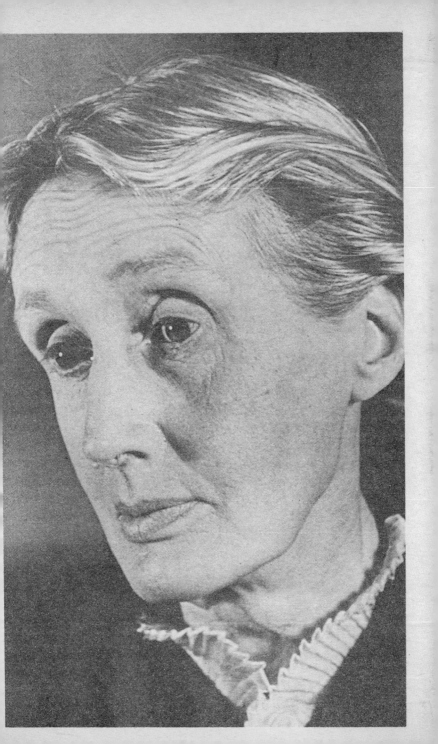

Top: View from Virginia Woolf's writing-room in the garden
at Monks House across the water-meadows to the Sussex Downs
Above: Godrevy lighthouse, St Ives Bay, prompted the symbolic
setting for *To the Lighthouse*

Leonard Woolf

Virginia Woolf

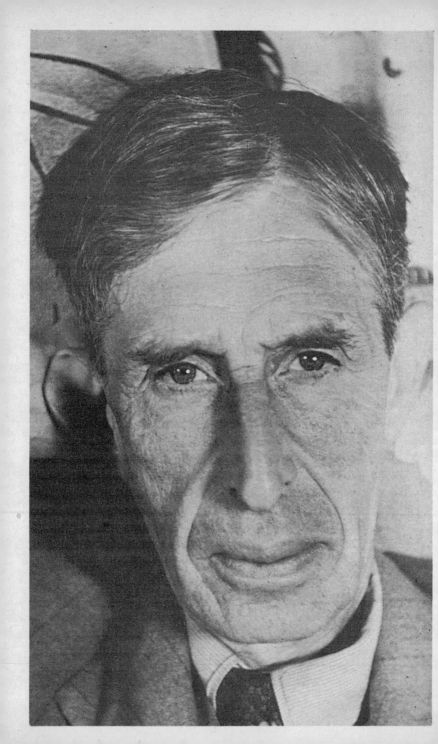

T. S. Eliot

IT has only been under peculiar conditions that I have ever been able to interest myself in criticizing – except in the currents of conversation – contemporary writers. In the case of authors whose work one considers pernicious, or whose work has been treated with an uncritical adulation which is pernicious, one figures to oneself occasionally an obligation to denounce or ridicule. In the case of authors whose merits have been ignored or misunderstood there is sometimes a particular obligation of championship. But when an author of unquestionable importance has received due tribute, and is not in the slightest danger of being overlooked or belittled, there is no compulsion to criticize: what chiefly matters is that his writing should be read. As soon as one generation has been succeeded by another, the endless labour of revaluations which will be in turn revalued must begin. It is not at the moment when a particular author dies that this work begins, but when a whole generation is gone.

There must, however, be some right point of reference for the moment of death, other than that of the formal obituary which is at best an attempt to say too much in too little space. It seems to me that when a great writer dies – unless he has already long outlived his life – something is in danger of vanishing which is not to reappear in the critical study, the full-length biography, or the anecdotal reminiscences. Perhaps it is something that cannot be preserved or conveyed: but at least we can try to set down some symbols which will serve to remind us in future that there is something lost, if we cannot remember what; and to remind a later generation that there is something they do not know, in spite of all their documents, even if we cannot tell them what. It is something which Virginia Woolf, with all her craft and genius, failed to convey in her life of Roger Fry: and if she failed who, if anyone, should have been successful with a lesser figure, I doubt whether we can do much about her, however we try. It is what someone, I forget who, must have meant when he wandered about saying simply: 'Coleridge is dead.' I mean that it is neither regret that an author's work has come to an end nor desolation at the loss of a friend, for the former emotion can be expressed, and the latter one keeps to oneself; but the loss of something both more profound and more extensive, a change to the world which is also a damage to oneself.

While this feeling cannot be communicated, the external situation can to some extent be outlined. Any dead author of long ago, an author on whom we feel some peculiarly personal dependence, we know primarily through his work – as he would wish to be known by posterity, for that is what he cared about. But we may also search and snatch eagerly at any anecdote of private life which may give us the feeling for a moment of seeing him as his contemporaries saw him. We may try to put the two together, peering through the obscurity of time for the unity which was both – and coherently – the mind in the masterpiece and the man of daily business, pleasure and anxiety as ourselves: but failing this, we often relapse into stressing the differences between the two pictures. No one can be understood: but between a great artist of the past and a contemporary whom one has known as a friend there is the difference between a mystery which baffles and a mystery which is accepted. We cannot explain, but we accept and in a way understand. It is this, I think, that disappears completely.

The future will arrive at a permanent estimate of the place of Virginia Woolf's novels in the history of English literature, and it will also be furnished with enough documents to understand what her work meant to her contemporaries. It will also, through letters and memoirs, have more than fugitive glimpses of her personality. Certainly, without her eminence as a writer, and her eminence as the particular kind of writer she was, she would not have occupied the personal position she held among contemporaries; but she would not have held it by being a writer alone – in the latter case it would only be the cessation of work which would here give cause for lament. By attempting to enumerate the qualities and conditions which contributed, one may give at first a false impression of 'accidental advantages' concurring to reinforce the imaginative genius and the sense of style which cannot be contested, to turn her into the symbol, almost myth, which she became for those who did not know her, and the social centre which she was for those who did. Some of these advantages may have helped to smooth the path to fame – though when a literary reputation is once established, people quickly forget how long it was in growing – but that fame itself is solidly enough built upon the writings. And these qualities of personal charm and distinction, of kindness and wit, of curiosity about human beings, and the particular advantage of a kind of hereditary position in English letters (with the incidental benefits which that position bestowed) do not, when enumerated, tell the whole story: they combined to form a whole which is more than the sum of the parts.

I am well aware that the literary-social importance which Virginia Woolf enjoyed had its nucleus in a society which those people whose ideas about it were vague – vague even in connection with the topography of London – were wont, not always disinterestedly perhaps, to deride. The sufficient answer *ad hoc* – though not the final answer – would probably be that it was the only one there was: and as I believe that without Virginia Woolf at the centre of it, it would have remained formless or marginal, to call attention to its interest to the sociologist is not irrelevant to my subject. Any group will appear more uniform, and probably more intolerant and exclusive from the outside than it really is; and here, certainly, no subscription of orthodoxy was imposed. Had it, indeed, been a matter of limited membership and exclusive doctrine, it would not have attracted the exasperated attention of those who objected to it on these supposed grounds. It is no part of my purpose here either to defend, criticize or appraise élites; I only mention the matter in order to make the point that Virginia Woolf was the centre not merely of an esoteric group, but of the literary life of London. Her position was due to a concurrence of qualities and circumstances which never happened before, and which I do not think will ever happen again. It maintained the dignified and admirable tradition of Victorian upper middle-class culture – a situation in which the artist was neither the servant of the exalted patron, the parasite of the plutocrat, nor the entertainer of the mob – a situation in which the producer and the consumer of art were on an equal footing, and that neither the highest nor the lowest. With the death of Virginia Woolf, a whole pattern of culture is broken : she may be, from one point of view, only the symbol of it; but she would not be the symbol if she had not been, more than anyone in her time, the maintainer of it. Her work will remain; something of her personality will be recorded : but how can her position in the life of her own time be understood by those to whom her time will be so remote that they will not even know how far they fail to understand it? As for us – *L'on sait ce que l'on perd. On ne sait jamais ce que l'on rattrapera.*

David Cecil

(Adapted from an interview
in the BBC Television film
A Night's Darkness. A Day's Sail)

Can you remember your very first meeting with Virginia Woolf?

I think it was at an evening party, given by a literary hostess called Miss Ethel Sands who lived in Chelsea. I was very excited because it was one of my first ventures into the literary world. I came into the room, where there were a lot of people, and saw two ladies sitting on a sofa at the back. Miss Sands led me up to them and introduced me. One was Mrs Harold Nicolson – Vita Sackville-West – the author, and the other was Virginia Woolf. I was already a very great admirer of Virginia Woolf's work. A lower, smaller chair was obtained for me and I sat looking up at these two goddesses.

And what transpired?

It was rather mortifying. Virginia Woolf was telling a story about something she'd read and describing it to Mrs Nicolson. She did this very well, and I sat open-mouthed with admiration. When she'd finished she turned and said, 'Now Lord David will tell us a story,' and looked at me. I felt absolutely unable to rise to the occasion. I hesitated and said, 'Oh, I've not read anything lately.' She said, 'But you must have read something.'

This made me seem very illiterate. So I began, crazily, telling the story of a novel that I'd been reading. It was much too long and I did it very badly, and after a minute or two I gave up, saying, 'I'm so sorry, I really can't go on, this is too boring – but it really is good when you read it.' She smiled at me rather ironically and said, 'I expect it would be better if one read it.' So my first interchange was rather chilling. On the other hand, I thought she looked marvellous, and as the evening went on, we got on, I think, very well.

Were there lots of examples in your relationship of this teasing and sometimes even of this malice? Did you see it at work?

Well, she was so very nice to me on the whole, but she was always a tease. She was like the child that puts its finger into the anemone to see if it'll close up. But she was always delightful. I once saw her rather too severe, but that time she was defeated.

Will you tell us about it?

It was later on, when I dined with her and Leonard. The other guest at that time was a lady novelist. After dinner, about ten o'clock, this lady's husband came in to fetch her. He was an unromantic figure, a philistine man with a toothbrush moustache and a square face. But he wanted to do his best: so he said, 'Are you writing anything now?' and she replied, 'I don't suppose you're very interested in writing,' with her ironical smile. He took that rather well. Then the conversation went on, and about a quarter of an hour later he said, 'I think we must go. I will have to go and wind up my car.' She said, 'What kind of a car have you got?' and he said, 'I don't suppose you're very interested in cars.' I thought he won that interchange. But she took it with a smile.

If you have any single image of her, any physical image, what is it?

Well ... two images I can think of. Physically she was very beautiful – in an old-fashioned, rather nineteenth-century style with an oval face and delicate features. She looked rather like a madonna. On the other hand there was something mocking in her, and amused. If you can imagine a mocking madonna, that's one image I have. The other is more of what her personality seemed like, not so much her face. I felt she was outside ordinary life. She was something more exquisite, more sensitive, more beautiful herself and more appreciative of beauty – but a little out of touch with the warmth of common humanity. She was rather like a mermaid. I thought she was like a beautiful mermaid who'd swum out of the sea to have a look at us all – very inquisitive, very interested. But like a mermaid.

Do you think that she really could be very warmly affectionate, or do you think there was always something withheld?

I didn't know her well enough to be sure about this. I can't really answer. But my impression is that she had very deep affections for her family. She wasn't cold-hearted or empty, she was withdrawn. Many people have told me that for her brothers and her sister, Vanessa, and her nephews and nieces she had a deep affection. And of course very much for Leonard.

Did you have the impression that she enjoyed talking to people and asking questions – all sorts of questions about their way of life and beliefs?

Virginia was an extraordinary unegostistic talker. She seemed much more interested in what other people said than in what she said herself. She questioned one a lot and seemed intensely interested in the answers. The questions were of all kinds, ranging from, 'What time does your mother have dinner?' – social customs interested her – to, 'Do you believe in God?' She seemed very surprised to find I believed in religion.

Did this, in a way, conform to the Bloomsbury Group's views on religion?

Yes. Bloomsbury was curiously cut off from the whole subject, far more than some other agnostics I have known. Its rationalism had a provincial quality about it. I don't think this was natural to Virginia. She had a vein in her imagination which it would perhaps be exaggerated to call mystical, but it was certainly incongruous with strict rationalism. I remember saying to her that I thought a passage in *The Years* indicated some kind of transcendental belief in a reality outside time and space, and asking her if I was right. She said yes, without committing herself to any definite statement about it.

Could you say, is there any way of defining or categorizing Bloomsbury, particularly about its voice and some of its attitudes towards the rest of the world?

It was very unlike anything else. I don't know if she was quite typical, there was something more imaginative, more poetic about her. Though most of Bloomsbury was cultivated and sensitive, I don't think it was exactly poetical. It was a very solid group and, when I first went to a party there, I was very much aware of this. I don't think it is at all true to call them affected. It was like any close group – it had its mannerisms of voice and phrasing.

They had a rather breathless way of talking, and a very solemn face. This was a little alarming. When they shook hands they didn't smile, they just handed the hand. And if you didn't know them, this grave look and this limp handshake were not welcoming.

Do you think that Virginia Woolf was a genius?

Yes. Virginia was exactly my idea of what one means by a genius. For me, a genius means somebody who sees the world and is able to make other people see it in a different light to anyone else. Geniuses are what I've heard somebody else describe as before-and-after writers. Life is not the same after reading them as it has been before. I think she was in the most intense sense a genius. I don't think it was a very broad genius, but the light that she did shed was wholly her own, and it penetrated very deep. Certainly the world hasn't looked the same to me since I read her books. I read them at a very formative age, when I was up first as an undergraduate at Oxford, and they meant more to me at that time than any other books by a contemporary author. I thought there were others who in some ways might be greater. But none altered my viewpoint in the way that Virginia did.

Nigel Nicolson

ALTHOUGH I was grown up and serving in the Army when Virginia died, I think of her entirely in terms of my childhood. I saw her many times, always in the company of one or both my parents, chiefly my mother, both at Rodmell and at Long Barn, our house near Sevenoaks, which was my childhood home till we moved to Sissinghurst in 1930 when I was aged thirteen. Virginia came a great deal to Long Barn after she first got to know my mother, which was in 1924. The period of their greatest intimacy was in the second half of the 1920s, but they continued to see much of each other and to correspond right up until her death. She also used to write to my brother and me occasionally, but like all schoolboys we did not realize the value of letters and I am afraid that I have none of them now. I have read, however, all her letters to my mother, the originals of which are in New York Public Library.

I would frequently return from school to find Virginia at Long Barn or Sissinghurst. She was marvellous with children. She treated us like grown-ups, looking upon childhood as yet another facet of human character. There was something in a child which no adult could recover; she was determined to discover what that special thing was. She used to interrogate us a great deal about the minutiae of our simple lives. It became a game; she was always interrupting us to say that we weren't being sufficiently precise in the little incidents of school life that we recounted to her.

I remember once coming home from Eton to find her at Sissinghurst. She asked me what had happened to me that day. I replied, 'Well, nothing has happened. I have just come home from school and here I am.' She said, 'Oh! that won't do, start at the beginning. What woke you up?' I said, 'It was the sun – the sun coming through the window of my room at Eton.' Then she said, leaning forward very intently, 'What sort of sun was it? Was it a cheerful sun or was it an angry sun?' In this sort of way we continued to retrace my day minute by minute: washing before breakfast, breakfast, packing, then the train journey and the switch from one station to another, up to the moment when I walked in at the door and found her there.

That was very typical of her. She was half collecting copy, because no human experience was considered by her too trivial to be interesting and she stored it away in the back of her mind; it might or might not come out years later in some totally changed way in one of her books. Virginia had this way of magnifying one's simple words and experiences. One would hand her a bit of information as dull as a lump of lead. She would hand it back glittering like diamonds. I always felt on leaving her that I had drunk two glasses of an excellent champagne. She was a life-enhancer. That was one of her own favourite phrases. She always said that the world was divided into two categories: those who enhanced life and those who diminished it.

My visits to Rodmell are all rather blurred together in my memory, but a very definite impression of the character of that household remains in my mind. It was rambling; it was untidy; it was a hugger-mugger of a house. Her own writing-room at the top of the house, which she used alternately with the pavilion in the garden, was really a horrid room but with a lovely view over the water-meadows.

There was very little apparent order in Virginia and Leonard's way of life, and no positive attempt to surround themselves with beautiful objects. There were paintings by Duncan Grant mixed up with coloured postcards from friends in Italy. There was a mass of books upon the shelves, lying stacked upon the floor, upon the staircase. A lot of dogs and cats, a lot of coming and going of domestics (although I think there was only one), but it always seemed there was a great bustle about the place, succeeded by periods of intense calm and concentration.

I can see Virginia now sitting beside her fireplace at Rodmell, rather on the edge of her chair, giving the impression of great alertness and eagerness to seize anything almost like a chameleon, as if she was about to dart out her tongue to pick up a phrase or reminiscence or an aspect of somebody's character. Very much alive and yet, combined with that, very great gentleness. The effect of gentleness came from two sources mainly. One was the immense grace of her movements and her whole appearance. Even as a child she struck me as being very beautiful, and I think that it was in her that I first came to appreciate the distinction between prettiness and beauty. Virginia was never pretty, but she remained very beautiful.

Her grace of deportment was very apparent to us. For instance, when she stood against a doorway it would always be with a sort of *S* curve of her slender body. She had this instinctive elegance, this natural poise, and her movements were very slow and tender. I remember one gesture in particular: she would remove a stray lock of hair – she had very long hair – from her forehead with her hand turned inward. A very slow movement of which she was quite unconscious, but which gave point to her conversation. almost a commentary upon it.

The second thing was her voice. Her voice was like old red velvet; it had extraordinary depth. On the telephone it could be mistaken for a man's voice. It had humour in it. A faint touch of malice, because there was certainly an element of malice in Virginia's character, rather, one might say, teasing, joking. Not always very kind about people when they weren't there. Always very kind to them when they were. She had a sharp wit which could be devastating. She never varied her manner between grown-ups or children. She would talk to us as though we were her adult contemporaries, and speak absolutely frankly about people whom we knew. There was always a great deal of laughter. It was a very gay household.

I remember one particular evening at Rodmell. I must have been about sixteen. Besides my mother, my brother and myself, the only other people were Virginia and Leonard, Maynard Keynes and his wife, Lydia Lopokova. Although I cannot recall a single word of the conversation, I do remember going away feeling that this is what life ought to be, this is what friendship really means. The visit made a great effect upon me; the gentleness and the wit, the humour, liveliness and the immense curiosity. I suppose that is really what Virginia contributed to my own outlook on life: her curiosity; nothing in the world was dull.

It wasn't her but my father – it could so easily have been her – who once said: 'Only one person in a thousand is a bore and he is interesting because he is one person in a thousand.' That was Virginia's attitude. Of course she could find people boring, but she was always predisposed to find them interesting.

Her relationship with Leonard had an almost biblical tenderness, like Mary and Joseph. They were utterly devoted to each other. In a way, their marriage was not unlike my own parents' marriage. Each partner to the two marriages was totally different from the other and yet they fused beautifully. You could see that Leonard was concerned the whole time that Virginia was all right, that she was not getting bored or tired. I think he describes it himself in his autobiography, as if he were looking after a very precious Ming vase which was known once to have been slightly cracked and which must be handled with immense care.

They complemented each other in a wonderful way. Virginia had no interest in politics, but politics was everything to Leonard. Leonard never pretended to be a creative writer. Yet each understood perfectly the other's perplexities. Even I as a boy appreciated this when I saw them together.

I thought of Virginia as more of a town person than a country person, more as an indoor than outdoor person, more as an evening than a daytime person. I don't quite know why this should be so. It partly derives, I suppose, from the fact that her occupation was a sedentary one. She wasn't very strong. Although she loved the garden at Rodmell, it obviously wasn't the centre of her life as the garden at Sissinghurst was to my mother. I see Virginia, if I could characterize her in a sentence, as somebody sitting beside a fire in an autumn evening, stretching out those long, thin, very beautiful hands to the flames to get warm. She always needed warmth, one felt, both in the physical sense and in the sense of companionship. She gave out a great deal of warmth, but she wanted it returned.

As children we realized, of course, that she was a person of very exceptional talent. The word genius was not much used in Bloomsbury circles, but my parents were always referring to her in a way in which they would refer to nobody else. Virginia was very very special. We knew that *Orlando* was a fantastic biography of my mother. It was illustrated in the later pages by photographs of her; there was never any pretence about it. When *Orlando* was being written, I can remember Virginia visiting Knole so that she could absorb the atmosphere for the novel. I was, I suppose, about eight then, and we have a photograph taken on that occasion.

I think that this really sums up my recollections of her. You can see there is not a lot of hard fact in what I have said. She was a background to our life, like a tapestry One didn't expect presents from her She once gave me a copy of *Flush* but that was the only thing, I think, that she ever gave me tangibly. But she gave us a new interest in life, a new way of looking at life. She amused us. She petted us as children. In her strange way I think she was rather fond of us, and we responded to her affection. Even at this distance in time, I can say without any exaggeration she was the most remarkable human being I have ever known.

Vita Sackville-West

(Written as a letter to a friend at the
time of Virginia Woolf's death, 1941)

Dear Elizabeth,

I feel sure that you must share my irritation at the
labels so persistently tied on to Virginia. Arnold Bennett,
I believe, was one of the first culprits: 'Queen of Bloomsbury', 'Queen of the Highbrows' and so on. It is thus in
anger that I take a pen to protest against so rigid a pigeon-
holing of so fluid a personality. For the term highbrow is
not usually applied in any complimentary sense. It is not
intended to define a rightly fastidious taste, but rather to
suggest a limited, carping attitude of mind; a mutual-
admiration society peculiar to a closed set; a languid outlook from which a warmer humanity is excluded. Recently it has given much satisfaction to many worthy
people to read about the Eclipse of the Highbrow, whatever that may mean; but certainly the only time I ever
thought of Virginia as being eclipsed was when the sun
himself shared her darkening, and I saw her standing
wraithlike on a Yorkshire moor while the shadow swept
onwards towards totality.

No, the wielders of rough judgement like Arnold Bennett and the readers of the correspondence in *The Times*
would be better advised to differentiate between highbrow and highbrow. It is the fake highbrow who has
given the bad name to the genuine. I need hardly remark

to you that Virginia was genuine all through. Any suggestion of pose (a crude and ill-considered word to throw at anybody, anyway) becomes ludicrous in association with a person so very much all of a piece. It was not even necessary to know her intimately to realize that she could not be otherwise than she was. One needed only to receive a postcard arranging or confirming an appointment to see that here was a mind with a twist of its own; always some quip or some unexpected phrase. I dare say you may remember the publication, many years ago, of a book called *The Bromide Book*. It is out of print and out of memory now, but it should be revived (perhaps as a Penguin or as one of the new Guild Books) as a salutary corrective for all those people who accept their opinions at second hand. The classification lay between Bromides and Sulphides: the dull bodies and the live wires. One applied the test to one's acquaintances and friends, and found that they responded to the test as readily as an electric battery responds to the touch of positive or negative. There was no half-way house. Virginia, even on the briefest postcard, was sulphidic. She was always herself; never anybody else at second hand.

Margot Oxford (herself a Sulphide) made one pertinent remark in the note which she contributed to *The Times*. 'What was curious about Virginia,' she wrote, 'was that her handwriting, countenance, and conversation were inseparably the same; equally sensitive and equally distinguished.' That is very true; and distinguished is, of course, one of the adjectives which can hardly be kept out of any comment. A little crowd of them comes trooping along: distinguished, fastidious – they all belong to the same family. There was a unity about her whole personality which instantly proposed such definitions. It is not going too far to suggest that her very name seemed made for her: Virginia Woolf. She could not have been better called, and was fortunate both as a baby at the font and in her marriage. Tenuousness and purity were in her baptismal name, and a hint of the fang in the other.

But it is not on these aspects of our uncommon friend that I intended to dwell. They could all be amplified by any intelligent reader. What I wished to recall to you who knew her, and to indicate if possible for those who knew of her only as a public character, was the enormous sense of fun she had (her own brand, certainly, as everything about her was her own brand), and the rollicking enjoyment she got out of easy things.

I don't know whether you will agree with this. Perhaps you will condemn this interpretation as shallow and will reply that for you she remains veiled in the slight romantic haze which surrounds a nature deepened by thoughtfulness and melancholy. It would be a falsity to deny this element in anyone who wrote the books she wrote, and you may go further and tell me that your impression is increased by the recollection of the hours one spent with her sitting in the half-light she loved, when her moving hands became shadowy and the teasing note left her voice and her features became visible only when she bent forward to poke the fire. Twilight and firelight were her own illumination; I will give you that. But at least you will agree that mental excitement was always the keynote. In the adventures of the mind she was a tireless treasure-seeker, whether she turned out the contents of her own imagination as an Elizabethan lumber-chest or cork-screwed into the recesses of one's own disposition. (What a knack she had for doing that! A common criticism of her novels was that she 'could not portray human beings', and indeed she could also weave fabulous tapestries out of her peculiar vision of her friends, but at the same time I always thought her genius led her by short cuts to some essential point which everybody else had missed. She did not walk there: she sprang.)

If you will concede that mental excitement was a key-note of her life, with all its implications and in all its forms, simple and complicated, so far removed from the popular conception of the languid destructive highbrow, you will agree also that she lived permanently like a poet on the plane where he finds himself enabled to produce poetry. An all-too-rare and infrequent state of mind, as any poet will tell you. But Virginia seemed able to sustain it in daily life. Technically speaking, she chose prose as her medium, not poetry, but that, surely, was by chance; a novel such as *The Waves* is pure poetry save for the fact that it happens to be written in prose. (Sir Thomas Browne figures here, I think, for she had a great dash of the seventeenth century in her.) Moreover, as she probably told you often, the idea of writing poetry did tempt her; the idea of combining poetry and fiction always allured her; and a careful reader may discover a buried versification of an unorthodox sort in at least one of her published works.

But this letter to you was not intended to turn into a critical essay on her works or her future intentions. It was intended to be a personal letter from one friend to another. Yet there is one thing I cannot refrain from asking you: Did the analogy between Virginia and Coleridge ever strike you? Did it ever occur to you that Virginia, translated into another century, might have written *Kubla Khan*, the *Ancient Mariner*, and the *Biographia Literaria*? She and Coleridge both seem to me to combine the unusually mixed ingredients of genius and intellect, the wild, fantastic, intuitive genius on the one hand, and the cold, reasoning intellect on the other. One difference between them was that Coleridge depended largely on the stimulation of opium for the exercise of his poetical genius. Virginia depended only on the stimulation which her own mind supplied. She was very temperate in her outward life. She liked wine, but drank it seldom; she liked it chiefly for its romantic quality, for its colour held up to the light; and for the heightening she so infrequently allowed it to give to her sensibilities.

She used to come and stay with me in an old cottage where the beams were already on the slant. I would give her a glass of Spanish wine the colour of red amber, and she would pretend that the beams went even more crooked after she had drunk it. It fitted in with her imagination to see things aslant rather than dully straight.

This was getting her away from her own background, the background of London and what is called Bloomsbury; from the background, even, of Monks House and the life that really fed her roots. So, finally, I come round to the Virginia I wanted to write to you about, the Virginia with whom I went alone to France.

She loved travelling. She was as excited as a schoolgirl on arriving in Paris. We went out after dinner and found a bookseller's shop open, and she perched on a stool and talked to the old bookseller about Proust. Next day we went south to Burgundy. There she forgot all about Proust in the simple enjoyment of the things we found. A fair in a French village, roundabouts, shooting-galleries, lions and gipsies giving a performance together, stalls with things to buy; all was sheer fun. We bought knives and green corduroy coats with buttons representing hares, pheasants, partridges. They were said to be gamekeepers' coats, but Virginia preferred to think that they were poachers'. The poacher would naturally be dearer to her mind than the keeper.

Then we went on from the village to the little towns, Avallon, Auxerre, and found the cathedral with its stained glass or the curiosity shop with its junk, and she discovered something in both. I never knew which she preferred, I think they each satisfied some demand in her mind, the kaleidoscopic beauty of the stained glass with its night-blues and yellows and reds, and the muddle of the junk shop where one might find a dressing-table or a 'Semaine Sainte' exquisitely leather-bound with the arms of Philippe d'Orléans for a few francs.

Then we went on to Vézelay and stayed there. You know all about Vézelay; Pater wrote about it. He is too wordy, as usual, too elaborately wordy; but when he calls Vézelay 'this iron place', and describes its church as 'a long massive chest there, heavy above you', he comes somewhere near to a true picture. In this iron place we stayed, hanging above the vineyards and the valley of the Cure. Virginia liked sitting among the vines or going for walks among the unfamiliar French lanes, but what I remember most vividly is one night when a superb thunderstorm broke over Vézelay and we sat in darkness while the flashes intermittently lit up her face. She was, I think, a little frightened, and perhaps that drove her to speak, with a deeper seriousness than I had ever heard her use before, of immortality and personal survival after death.

One note I will add to show once more how human she was. Her French wasn't good, although she could read it easily and had walked round and round Tavistock Square, practising aloud the conversation she was learning by gramophone records. In France with me she had refused to utter a word, and the only phrase I ever heard came to my ears when it wasn't meant to. It was on the boat as we put out from Dieppe to Newhaven. Rather apprehensively she had approached a sailor: *'Est-ce que la mer est brusque?'*

Well . . . I seem to have put very little into this letter, probably because there was too much to say. But if I have corrected any misapprehensions (not in your mind, for I am certain they did not exist there), I shall feel rewarded.

Yours ever,
V. Sackville-West

George Rylands

(Adapted from an interview
in the BBC Television film
A Night's Darkness. A Day's Sail)

*One of the things that I find the most difficult of all to
understand about Virginia Woolf is how she managed
to combine this extraordinary literary output, both of
creative writing and journalism, with being often a very
ill woman. Were you at all aware in your friendship with
her of how ill she was?*

No. I mean, I knew about the troubles before I went
to the Hogarth Press. I knew about the great illness and
the attempted suicide and so on, and I knew that she
could get highly strung up and over-excited. Leonard
Woolf kept a sharp eye on all this, about whether she
should go out to a party and what social life she should
have, particularly of course when she was in the middle
of one of her works and was in a state of regular inspiration. But one can tell from the *Writer's Diary* that she
was one of those writers who, when they are writing,
move into some other world altogether. They are in a
state of trance almost. But of course I think this is one
of the reasons why she felt the greatest admiration for
Shakespeare and felt something in common with him.
He wrote with this extreme rapidity, and she also when
she was working worked at that rate absolutely – it came
hot like lava from her. Then of course she went back

over it, and went back over it again, and over it again, until at last when it had gone to the printers then she had this terrible reaction because she could not yet again take it and go through it. But I think that she was in this state of trance and it was therefore not a question of being ill or not, except that you can say that mystics and people who write in that kind of way are in a trance. Not in the way that, say, Somerset Maugham wrote, or Trollope wrote, which is a job – a professional thing – in which you know exactly how to do your profession. But she was one of those people, like the poets and the painters and musicians, who is inspired.

You would say then that she was a genius?

Oh, undoubtedly. A genius in a sense in which I cannot really think of anybody else in my own time. A genius in literature – well, Lawrence, but I never met D. H. Lawrence. He was of course clearly a genius. Whether he was a good writer or not, he was a genius. I wouldn't say that Lytton Strachey was a genius, or any other of the Bloomsbury people in writing – unless, perhaps, E. M. Forster.

T. S. Eliot?

Yes, undoubtedly a genius.

Yeats?

Yes. I only met Yeats once or twice. Yes, a genius – the greatest. And Hardy I met. I went to tea with Hardy about 1927, I think. But then of course Hardy and Yeats are the older generation. I was thinking more of Virginia's own generation. But Joyce, of course, we would have to say that he was a genius. It would be terrible not to mention Joyce, wouldn't it? Especially now he's in paperback.

Perhaps it would be helpful if you could define what you mean by genius?

No, I don't think so. We know perfectly well that there are some people who, as I say, are in a state of trance when they are creative. They don't know what they are doing or why they are doing it. It almost can become automatic writing – as it did with someone like Swinburne, for instance.

Would you agree with something that her nephew and biographer, Quentin Bell, said: that she was a woman who was perpetually trembling on the edge of ecstasy?

Yes. I should have thought that she very often went *over* the edge. I should have thought very often when she was perhaps looking at a picture or hearing a piece of music, or responding to something in the country. You can't tremble on the edge of ecstasy, either you have ecstasies or you don't.

When you went to Rodmell – what was it like staying there?

The simple life, you know, what Wordsworth called humble and rustic life. Nothing, of course, could be more agreeable. Sussex is very beautiful – or at any rate it was then. There was the garden, not so remarkable as it is now. Leonard Woolf became a dedicated gardener. But when I first went to Rodmell it was quite simple – and delightful. Virginia used to go off to her hut in the garden and disappear, and then in the afternoon we went for walks. There was one terrible time when we were going over to see Maynard and Lydia Keynes, who lived nearby at Tilton. Leonard Woolf asked me if I could drive a pony and trap. I was too shy to say I couldn't and so I said yes. Then Virginia and I were put into the trap and we set off for Tilton, about ten miles away – Leonard followed behind us on a bicycle – then of course I found that I couldn't control the horse. We were trying to go down a steep hill among the Sussex Downs and the horse ran away. Leonard got into a frenzy, leaped off his bicycle and ran and took the reins. Then, as far as I can remember, he drove the trap and I got on the bicycle. It was not very satisfactory, but you can see that was a world in which there were not many motor-cars on the roads, but a horse and trap or a pony-cart.

Can you describe to me what the parties were like in the Bloomsbury days?

In those days after the end of the first war there was a frenzied kind of excitement and relief from everything. The parties were mostly fancy-dress parties, and there were charades, and people wrote plays for them. They went on absolutely all night, and were very enjoyable. I can remember a marvellous party, called the Sailors' Party, in which we all had to go wearing naval costume. I went as a lower-deck type, and Lytton went as a full Admiral of the Fleet. As you can imagine, with his beard and his cocked hat and his sword he was impressive. Well then, there used to be parties given by the Keynes's at which we did theatricals, and Keynes used to appear as the Prince Consort and his wife, Lopokova, as Queen Victoria. On one occasion I wrote a satirical account of what went on in the Hogarth Press basement, the series of people who had been there and only lasted six months and been thrown out – of which I, needless to say, proved to be one. I wrote it as a little sketch, which we did, and I think it was taken all right by the Woolfs. And then there was another party that I gave with two other friends at which we had about two hundred people. I was lodging with Douglas Davidson, a painter and close Cambridge friend, at the top of the house in Gordon Square kept by Duncan and Vanessa. They let us the two top floors. At this party we had an immense gathering of everybody we knew: the ballet, and Margot Asquith, Mary Pickford, Lady Ottoline Morrell, and all Bloomsbury and everything else. There was nothing much to eat except heaps of strawberries and cream and cheap white wine. We didn't mind much in those days what we ate and drank as long as there was plenty of everything. On that occasion there came a very famous popular novelist called Berta Ruck, whom you may 'never even have heard of. Although not as famous as Ethel M. Dell she belonged to the Ethel M. Dell world of best-sellers, and she was awfully jolly. I think she was married to a best-seller writer called Oliver Onions – however, be that as it may, she came.

The party spread all over the house, and up in my bedroom which was a sort of attic room – Berta was there with me and with Virginia. There was a certain complication about their meeting because in one of her books Virginia describes walking through a cemetery – perhaps it was in *To the Lighthouse* – and looking at the names on the graves and one of the names she mentioned was Berta Ruck. Virginia hadn't the faintest idea who Berta Ruck was – who sold, I suppose, five hundred times more copies of her novels every year than Virginia ever sold. But the name stuck in her mind so when she was writing an account of names in this cemetery she read Berta Ruck on one of the tombstones. Well, as you can imagine, the publishers got on to it and Berta Ruck got on to it and Oliver

Onions got on to it. It was settled out of court and everything was all right, but here they were meeting up in my attic for the first time. They were amicable and everything was perfectly happy and gay and noisy – there must have been about a dozen of us up there. Then Berta Ruck treated us to an Edwardian popular song of which the theme was, 'I never allow a sailor an inch above my knee', which she sang with dance steps and lifting her skirt to make the point. Of course nowadays you couldn't do it any more, but in those days skirts came half-way down the calf and so she could lift it and show her knees, and very exciting it was. And there was Virginia sitting absolutely entranced and rapt by the whole thing. Of course the great thing about Bloomsbury was that they had no nonsense about impropriety, I mean you really could say anything. In fact, it took me quite a long time not to be shocked by their conversation. Not that I was shocked by Berta Ruck singing 'I never allow a sailor an inch above my knee.'

Would you describe your rooms at King's and the luncheon party when Virginia and Leonard Woolf came down to see you at Cambridge?

Well, I think it was in 1928 when Virginia came down to read a paper to Newnham and to Girton about how women were so 'deprived' – as it is now called – as far as educational opportunities were concerned. I had been made a Fellow in about 1927 and had been in these rooms for about a year, this being part of what had been the Provost's Lodge. Then a new Provost's Lodge had been built and I was allowed to come into these rooms because they were going to pull the whole building down and therefore no senior Fellow wanted them. They let me have the use of the rooms, which was going to be for two years and has in fact been forty-two years. Anyway, Virginia was coming down to read these papers and of course I asked her and Leonard to come and have lunch with me. At that time there were very few possessions in the north room, which is a large room. It had a table and chairs and a few other bits and pieces, but nothing compared with now. On that account I had asked Carrington, who was the great friend of Lytton Strachey – Carrington Partridge as she was then – if she would come down and decorate the rooms for me so that they would be less bare and bleak. She came down and stayed two or three days and painted the four doors in the four corners of the room, and the fireplace, and made it look like a really civilized and delightful room.

It was to this room that Leonard and Virginia came – I don't doubt that I had two or three other people, perhaps Forster, to lunch to meet them – and that lunch is described, in the fantasy world in which Virginia always described things, in her book *A Room of One's Own*. It goes as follows:

... I shall take the liberty to defy the convention and tell you that the lunch on this occasion began with soles, sunk in a deep dish, over which the college cook had spread a counterpane of the whitest cream, save that it was branded here and there with brown spots like the spots on the flanks of a doe. After that came the partridges, but if this suggests a couple of bald, brown birds on a plate you are mistaken. The partridges, many and various, came with all their retinue of sauces and salads, the sharp and the sweet, each in its order; their potatoes, thin as coins but not so hard; their sprouts, foliated as rosebuds but more succulent. And no sooner had the roast and its retinue been done with than the silent serving-man, the Beadle himself perhaps in a milder manifestation, set before us, wreathed in napkins, a confection which rose all sugar from the waves. To call it pudding and so relate it to rice and tapioca would be an insult. Meanwhile the wine-glasses had flushed yellow and crimson; had been emptied; had been filled. And thus by degrees was lit, half-way down the spine, which is the seat of the soul, not that hard little electric light which we call brilliance, as it pops in and out upon our lips, but the more profound, subtle, and subterranean glow which is the rich yellow flame of rational intercourse. No need to hurry. No need to sparkle. No need to be anybody but oneself. We are all going to heaven and Vandyck is of the company ...

Well, I'm glad it seemed like that to Virginia – perhaps not so much, I expect, to Leonard. It seemed like that to me, this was glamour and romance. But, partridges *various*? I don't think there could be more than one kind of partridge. And I don't very much like the idea, except that it was very much like college cooking, of a counterpane of sauce with some little brown flecks on it. Never mind. And I hope there were *two* wines. I think it unlikely and there was probably only one. Anyway, as when she describes Bond Street in *Mrs Dalloway* or when she desscribes an herbaceous border in which all the flowers in all the seasons bloom at the same time, as always with Virginia it is the idealized, the romantic fantasy of what should have been and what it was to her. And what it certainly was to me.

Barbara Bagenal

I KNEW Virginia's sister, Vanessa Bell, before I met Virginia. I first met Vanessa in the autumn of 1913 at one of Ottoline Morrell's Thursday evening parties at her home in Bedford Square. I do not remember seeing Virginia and Leonard there at any time, but I am sure they must have joined in occasionally. Many of us who went to these parties were greatly influenced by the Russian Ballet and we often went to Ottoline's house straight from Covent Garden. Philip Morrell played the pianola for us and we all danced madly together – probably still influenced by the ballet. They were great gatherings. We had long discussions, endless arguments and tremendous fun.

I think that Vanessa was interested in me because I was, for those days, a very independent young woman. I had a passionate wish to draw and paint and had lived in a hostel in Paris so that I could draw all day and every day at the Grande Chaumière Académie. By the time I met her, I was studying at the Slade School and living on my own in a studio in Hampstead – a state of feminine liberation which I think intrigued her.

Vanessa and I became lifelong friends.. When I came to know her well I found that she was able to get through a tremendous amount of work in her studio because her daily routine was so well organized. This applied to Virginia too. They would not let anything interfere with their working routines and set special hours aside each day. At that time, of course, domestic help was readily available; at her home in Gordon Square Vanessa had a cook, a housemaid and two nurses for the children. At Hogarth House in Richmond Virginia had two maids, Nellie and Lottie. All of whom, I am sure, helped them both to keep so methodically to their time-tables.

One of my early meetings with Virginia and Leonard was in 1916 when Saxon Sydney-Turner and I were invited to dinner at Hogarth House. Saxon and Leonard had been at Cambridge together, they were contemporaries at Trinity and had remained friends after they came down. Saxon was a very reserved man, sometimes hardly speaking at all to anyone he did not know well, but Virginia was devoted to him and managed to make him almost voluble. She loved talking to him and asking searching questions about music – a subject which he had studied all his life. In fact he, Virginia and her brother Adrian went to many operas and concerts together. Saxon was an insatiable reader and would read Greek or Latin until the early hours of the morning. He won prizes for solving crosswords and making acrostic puzzles in Latin verse because he could retain facts rather like an encyclopedia. Virginia was fascinated by his extraordinary mind, his accumulation of knowledge and his very odd character. I remember her telling me that she went to see him one day when he was ill in bed – he was living in two furnished rooms in Great Ormond Street – and while talking to him she suddenly noticed two similar pictures on the walls. They were rather hideous oleographs of a farm scene. She said, 'Saxon, you have exactly the same picture each side of your bed!' This news didn't surprise him at all. He was silent for a moment, then said,

'Oh really, have I?' She said to me, 'There will *never* be his like again. He is unique.'

After several meetings with Virginia I noticed that one of her characteristics was to ask innumerable questions. She was intensely interested in what people were thinking and why. It was not just an inquisitive interest, she really wanted to understand everyone's mind and thoughts. I felt that by asking so many questions she was making notes for her work as a writer the whole time. She was also a very gay and amusing person, sometimes with a slightly malicious edge to her humour, but her gaiety was accompanied by an enlivening nervous energy that encouraged everyone to respond.

Virginia was very beautiful; she had an aquiline face, a wide forehead and large green eyes. But she had a strange, rather clumsy way of moving. She was not as graceful as Vanessa. There was one similarity, however: her voice, like Vanessa's, was low, melodious and distinctive.

I came to know Virginia well when in 1917 I went to help her and Leonard set up type at the Hogarth Press – if in those days it could be called by so professional a name. They had started the Press mainly as a hobby for Virginia. It was intended to help her to relax when she was concentrating too hard on her work. Even when not sitting at her desk she was still thinking about the novel she was writing, and this intense concentration brought on acute headaches and sometimes led to a serious mental breakdown.

Leonard had bought a small hand-press, type, frames and a book of instructions for printing. Thus equipped they had set up their first publication, *Two Stories*, and had included in the book some small woodcut illustrations which they had asked a friend of mine, Carrington, to do for them. Carrington and I had been at the Slade together and afterwards, of course, she became Lytton Strachey's great friend. Early in 1917 we had spent many weeks bicycling round the countryside looking for a house for Lytton. We found one eventually, the Mill House, at Tidmarsh, where he was able to work undisturbed by the noise of war-time London and to finish writing *Eminent Victorians*.

After completeing their first book for the Hogarth Press Leonard and Virginia had run into difficulties. Neither of them was practical, they were not good at using their hands like professional craftsmen and so they found that their book contained a number of printing mistakes. They decided that they needed help with the typesetting and asked a friend, Alix Sargant-Florence, if she would do this work for them. Alix went to Hogarth House and tried setting up type, but found it was much too tedious an occupation and resigned after the first day. Then they asked Vanessa if she knew of anyone who could help, and Vanessa suggested me. At this time, the summer of 1917, I was camping out in the rickyard at Charleston, the Bells' farmhouse near Lewes, and was doing some of the gardening with Vanessa. I agreed to help Virginia and Leonard with their type-setting and so, when I returned to Hampstead, Virginia came to tell me about the work. I remember her saying, 'You will have a season ticket to Richmond, a share of the profits on the publications, and lunch and tea.' Then she added, 'For lunch there will be meat, two veg and pudding!'

I worked three days a week at the Press and, in order to get there, travelled from Hampstead to Richmond in an old steam-train, then walked up the hill behind the station to Hogarth House in Paradise Road. It was a beautiful house, built in a simple Georgian style, with wide windows and a large white porch. When I arrived the first day I found that Virginia and Leonard had nearly finished binding *Two Stories*. For each copy, they had sewn the pages and a red and white cover together with a darning needle and thread. As there were more than 120 copies it must have been a very tough and tedious job and I think that Nellie and Lottie might well have helped with some of the sewing. Virginia and Leonard were then about to start on their second publication, which was Katherine Mansfield's story, *Prelude*. I did not want to hurt Leonard's feelings, but I noticed that the title-page of *Two Stories* was out of proportion and asked him if he would allow me to set up the title-page of *Prelude*. He was rather surprised at my criticism and very reluctant to let me do it, but in the end he agreed. And so I started work as an apprentice type-setter at the Hogarth Press – and the title-page of Katherine Mansfield's story became my own effort.

Every morning I set up type in a little room at the top of the house. It was next to Virginia's room where, starting promptly at 10 o'clock each day, she worked at her novel until lunchtime. At first I had some difficulties with my new job – for instance, I did not know how to divide the words at the end of a line of type – and I had to go into Virginia's room many times to ask her advice. But she did not mind being interrupted and solved my problems with an extraordinary amount of patience.

I enjoyed setting up type and was happy doing this work for many weeks. However, as winter approached I became increasingly aware that my little room was extremely cold. There was no fire in the room because coal was rationed and Leonard was very careful about using it. He mixed fireclay balls with the coal to make it last longer in the house and I felt diffident about asking him for a fire. Eventually I developed a very bad cold and had to stay away from the Press until it was better. Lytton Strachey came to see me one day in Hampstead and was amazed that I did not like to ask Leonard for a fire; he rang him at once and said it was monstrous not to put one in my room. Fortunately Leonard was not offended. When I returned to the Press he had a small fire lit for me each day.

Every afternoon Virginia helped me with the type-setting, and together we set most of the pages of *Prelude*. The very small type was difficult for Leonard to handle so he did the printing. Sometimes I helped him with this, but progress was slow because the small hand-press could take only one page at a time. After some weeks Leonard decided that we would have to change to a larger machine. He found a jobbing printer, McDermott, who owned a small firm near the Green in Richmond. McDermott had a treadle platen machine which printed four pages at a time and he was willing to let us use it. In order to do the work ourselves we had to lock four pages of *Prelude* into a chase belonging to him and then carry it down to the Green.

It was a much quicker way of printing, but it presented a difficult problem for me. I had to put the paper into the machine and, at the same time, press down a pedal with my foot. I was not tall enough to do both these movements at once and nearly fell into the machine as the frames came down on to the paper. Leonard, sensing some fearful accident, decided that he and McDermott would do the printing while Virginia and I finished the type-setting at the house.

At this time, the winter of 1917, we had another problem to face. It was not connected with the Press, but with the air raids that had increased in intensity during the last year of the war. Richmond has a distinctive white bridge over the Thames and it was an easy target for the German bombers at full moon. When an air-raid warning had been given, Virginia would not let me go home and insisted that I stayed at Hogarth House.

I particularly remember one noisy night when the bridge was bombed. I was sleeping on Virginia's rest couch in her room on the top floor and Leonard called out to me to bring my blankets down to the kitchen in the basement and make up a bed under the table. When I had staggered down with the bedding I found Virginia tucked into a camp-bed on one side of the range, Lottie and Nellie in an equally small bed on the other side, and Leonard, looking most unhappy, was lying on a mattress on top of the kitchen table. We tried to settle down, but the noise from the anti-aircraft guns was so intense that sleep was out of the question. We were all rather alarmed, especially Lottie and Nellie, but Virginia managed to make them laugh by joking about Leonard who was precariously balanced on top of the table. Leonard did not find the situation amusing at all; he felt responsible for our safety during the air raid and so silenced us from time to time with a very stern 'Be quiet!' I remember it as being a most extraordinary night.

Sometimes Leonard could be surprisingly censorious, as on this occasion. But he could also be very amusing. Usually he did not mind if we laughed now and then at his expense and would join in the laughter with us.

One afternoon, when he had been shopping in Richmond at a branch of the Co-operative Society – an organization which interested him enormously and which he supported whenever possible – he came home carrying a large paper parcel. While we were having tea he undid the parcel: it contained two enormous pairs of thick woollen combinations for Virginia. They had long legs, long sleeves, and an array of buttons. Virginia and I laughed at these extraordinary garments until there were tears in our eyes. I said, 'Leonard, I wouldn't be seen dead in one of those!' Fortunately he wasn't upset. He gazed long and thoughtfully at the combinations and then joined in the laughter too.

Because Leonard was so interested in the Co-operative movement, Virginia asked a group of elderly working women members to tea once a fortnight. They were a sort of mothers' meetings. She loved talking to these women and, of course, asking them innumerable questions so that she could learn as much as possible about their lives. They were all doing war work, which in most cases meant monotonous jobs in factories, and so, to make the tea parties especially interesting for them, she asked her friends to come and give talks. When I had married and left the Press, Virginia asked my husband, Nicholas, if he would give one of these talks. He told them about his experiences during the war and what it was like in the trenches in France. They were extremely interested in what he had to say – including Virginia, Lottie and Nellie – and the afternoon was a great success.

Prelude was published in 1918, after I was married. Later that year Virginia and Leonard came to tea with me in Hampstead and, true to his word, Leonard handed me my share of the profits. It was half a crown, handed to me shyly behind his back. Virginia said, 'Leonard, you *can't* give Barbara only two shillings and sixpence!' But that was my share of the profits in 1918. Then later, as an extra present, Leonard gave me a copy of *Prelude*. The cover was dark blue and the binding, I think, had been professionally done by McDermott. This copy is now one of my most cherished possessions.

It had been a great joy and privilege for me to have worked with Virginia for so long, and to have been the first apprentice type-setter at the Hogarth Press. Leonard and Virginia were such an unusual couple. They seemed to have so little in common, their characters were so different, and yet I cannot remember them having a quarrel all the time I was with them. Leonard was wonderfully patient with Virginia and completely devoted to her. It must have been a terrible strain for him to have guarded and protected her all the time from a mental fatigue that could overcome her so quickly and so disastrously.

Vanessa told me that during one of her earlier illnesses Virginia would not eat anything at all. Leonard and their friend Ka Cox had sat for hours each side of her bed patiently persuading her to eat. They managed to spoon-feed her a little at a time, but sometimes she would hit the spoon away, or occasionally would accept food only from Ka, or else only from Leonard.

When I was at Hogarth House the worst of these illnesses were over. Although Virginia was working with great concentration on her second novel, *Night and Day*, I saw her only once near to a mental breakdown. We were laughing and joking at lunch one day when suddenly she began to flip the meat from her plate on to the table-cloth, obviously not knowing what she was doing. Leonard at once asked me not to comment on her action and to stop talking to her. Then he took her upstairs to rest and stayed with her until she fell asleep and the danger was passed. At tea-time she was quite happy and composed and did not remember the incident.

I had always thought that a hobby would have been a great help to Virginia, it would have given her a much needed rest from her work. But she had no hobbies – other than the brief one of type-setting. She could not play the piano, or knit, or sew. And I was surprised to find that she could not cook – at least, not in the early years of her marriage. One week-end, when Virginia and Leonard were staying at Asheham, I walked over from Charleston to stay the night with them. When I arrived, Virginia said that she did not know what we could have for supper because the woman who came in to cook for them was ill. I suggested that I made some scrambled eggs. Virginia was amazed and said, 'Can you really cook scrambled eggs?'

I remember surprising her, too, on another occasion – though perhaps in rather a different way. Because she could not sew I had made a long overall for her so that the ink from the press would not get on to her clothes, and while I was fitting it on her I put some pins in my mouth. This horrified her. She said, 'Barbara, only professionals do that, it is very dangerous.'

There was in fact nothing of greater interest to Virginia than her work and it was impossible for her to let anything detract from this for very long. The only pastime she would indulge in was walking. It was her great joy. She loved going for long walks through the streets that she knew well in London, or over the Downs in Sussex. One afternoon, when I had been walking over the Downs with her, we were returning through Rodmell village and she saw a mass of tall yellow flowers growing in a cottage garden. She asked me the name of the flower. I knew it well and said at once, 'Tropaeolum Canaryensis'. The name delighted her and she was amused by my quick reply. 'Such a long name from so small a person,' she said. 'I shall call you Barbara Chickabiddyensis – I think it suits you.' And that became her nickname for me – not only when we met, but whenever she wrote a letter to me afterwards.

Virginia loved children, especially Vanessa's. I always

thought it was tragic that she could not have any of her own. Every Christmas holiday Vanessa gave a fancy-dress party in her studio in Fitzroy Street for Angelica. All the grown-ups joined in and enjoyed themselves enormously – particularly Virginia, who played the wildest games with the children. A small play was rehearsed each time for the party; one year it was adapted from Thackeray's story for children, *The Rose and the Ring*, and another from *Through the Looking-Glass*. I remember, in this play, Roger Fry took the part of the White Knight. He looked very amusing in a white flowing garment with colanders and saucepans sewn all over it. When the party was being planned Vanessa asked the children whom, of all their friends and relations, they particularly wanted to invite. They all shouted at once 'Virginia!' Like the children, I think it was her enormous sense of gaiety that one remembers most of all about her.

My daughter, Judith, who went to Angelica's parties, remembers too how amusing Virginia could be. When she was a child she met her one day in Lewes High Street. Virginia said to her, 'Will you come with me to Woolworth's to buy a very large india-rubber? I want to rub out all my novels.'

Louie Mayer

IN the summer of 1934, when I was living at Southease in Sussex, I saw an advertisement in a local newspaper that particularly interested me: it said that a cook-general was wanted at a small country house near Lewes and that living accommodation – a cottage – would be provided rent-free. Replies were to be sent to Mrs Woolf, Monks House, Rodmell. I was delighted to find this advertisement: it was the type of work I was looking for and my husband and I needed a cottage of our own. We also needed a school near by for our children. I knew there was one at Rodmell, so I replied to the advertisement at once.

When I posted the letter I thought that perhaps nothing would come of it. As had happened before, I might not even have a reply. But within a few days, to my surprise, both Mr and Mrs Woolf came to see me. They must have read the letter when they came down to Rodmell for the week-end and then driven the few miles to Southease early the next morning.

They described to me the work I would do at Monks House in great detail. Mr Woolf explained that their day was very carefully planned, almost hour by hour, and it was important nothing should happen that could alter their routine. I felt that they must be people who really loved time. Indeed I hoped that I would be able to keep to the hours they mentioned, but it did seem to be a rather alarming time-table. Mrs Woolf then told me about the cottage. It was only 'two up and two down' she said, but it was not far from the house and improvements would be made to it for whoever had the job.

A few days later Mrs Woolf wrote to me – I can remember the letter well, it was written on bright green paper – she said that she would engage me and to begin with would pay me seven shillings and sixpence a week and that I could live in the cottage Mr Woolf had bought in Rodmell. I was thrilled that the job was mine. In those days, seven shillings and sixpence a week and a cottage rent-free was really a big wage.

I was very young when I started work at Monks House and I wondered if I would be able to keep to so strict a time-table. I knew I could make a success of the job if I did the right thing at the right time. But I need not have worried: Mr and Mrs Woolf went to a lot of trouble to make me feel at home and help me adjust to their routine. I liked them both the very first week.

I had a long day's work, starting at eight in the morning and ending after nine at night, but in those days I – and my friends doing the same jobs – did not think of our day in terms of hours. We liked our work, we were proud to do it well, and I am afraid that we were very very happy. Although my husband also had an extremely busy day, he helped me by putting our two children to bed. I had some free time in the afternoon and was able to spend it with my family, but the children often came with me to Monks House. In fact I think they were practically brought up there in the kitchen; they ran in and out to the garden, helping Percy Bartholomew, Mr Woolf's gardener, as if it was their own home.

There was one thing I found rather strange on my first

day. The floors in Monks House were very thin, the bath-room was directly above the kitchen and when Mrs Woolf was having her bath before breakfast I could hear her talking to herself. On and on she went, talk, talk, talk: asking questions and giving herself the answers. I thought there must be two or three people up there with her. When Mr Woolf saw that I looked startled he told me that Mrs Woolf always said the sentences out loud that she had written during the night. She needed to know if they sounded right and the bath was a good, resonant place for trying them out. He was so used to hearing her talk to herself in this way that he did not notice it at all. I became used to it too, but it startled me in the mornings for quite some time.

I was not allowed to make coffee at Monks House – Mr and Mrs Woolf were very particular about coffee and always made it themselves – so Mr Woolf came into the kitchen at 8 o'clock every morning to make it. When we carried the breakfast trays to Mrs Woolf's room I noticed that she had always been working during the night. There were pencils and paper beside her bed so that when she woke up she could work, and sometimes it seemed as though she had had very little sleep. These pieces of paper, some of them containing the same sentence written over and over again, would be in heaps about the room. They were on the chairs, on the tables and sometimes even on the floor. It was one of Mrs Woolf's habits, when she was working, to leave her writing about in little heaps of paper. I would find them about the house too: in the sitting-room and dining-room on the tables and the mantelpieces.

Mrs Woolf's bedroom was always outside the house in the garden; I used to think how inconvenient it must be to have to go out in the rain to go to bed. She also had a writing-room in the garden, near her room, because it was quiet there and she could work undisturbed. Her bedroom had been added on to the back of the house; the door faced the orchard and a window at the side opened out on to a large field. I remember that a cow came one night and put its head in through the window. It amused Mrs Woolf very much, but in case it happened again Mr Woolf bought the field and added part of it to the garden. Then, because the writing-room was small, he had a larger one built for her at the end of the garden against the church wall. When it was finished, Mrs Woolf had a beautiful view eastwards across the meadows to Mount Caburn, and that is where she used to sit every day and work.

I can always remember her coming to the house each day from the writing-room: when I rang the bell for lunch at 1 o'clock she used to walk down through the orchard smoking one of her favourite cigarettes in a long holder. She was tall and thin and very elegant. She had large, deep-set eyes and a wide curving mouth – I think perhaps it was this feature that made her face seem particularly beautiful. She wore long skirts – usually blue or brown corduroy – in the fashion of the day, and silk jackets of the same colour. I remember, too, there was always a large silk handkerchief tucked into the jacket pocket.

Her cigarettes were made from a special tobacco called My Mixture. Mr Woolf bought it for her in London and, in the evenings, they used to sit by the fire and make these cigarettes themselves. It was a mild sweet-smelling tobacco, and she would not have any other cigarettes, though sometimes she smoked a long thin cheroot which she enjoyed very much.

Mrs Woolf wore clothes that suited her well, especially when she was going to a party. I pressed them for her and did any sewing that was necessary – she was not able to sew, although sometimes she liked to try. She liked trying to cook too, but I always felt that she did not want to give time to cooking and preferred to be in her room working.

But there was one thing in the kitchen that Mrs Woolf was very good at doing : she could make beautiful bread. The first question she asked me when I went to Monks House was if I knew how to make it. I told her that I had made some for my family, but I was no expert at it. 'I will come into the kitchen, Louie,' she said, 'and show you how to do it. We have always made our own bread.' I was surprised how complicated the process was and how accurately Mrs Woolf carried it out. She showed me how to make the dough with the right quantities of yeast and flour, and then how to knead it. She returned three or four times during the morning to knead it again. Finally, she made the dough into the shape of a cottage loaf and baked it at just the right temperature. I would say that Mrs Woolf was not a practical person – for instance, she could not sew or knit or drive a car – but this was a job needing practical skill which she was able to do well every time. It took me many weeks to be as good as Mrs Woolf at making bread, but I went to great lengths practising and in the end, I think, I beat her at it.

I soon became interested in preparing all sorts of dishes at Monks House. Mr and Mrs Woolf did not like me to cook large meals, but they lived well and enjoyed good food. They particularly liked game – grouse and pheasant with well-made sauces. Puddings had to be very light and newly made, they were mostly *crèmes* and *soufflés*. I became so interested in cooking that Mrs Wolf asked me if I would like to have lessons in advanced cooking at Brighton Technical College. I thought this was a wonderful idea, and so she arranged for me to have a year's course.

I enjoyed the lessons enormously; every day I left Rodmell at eleven in the morning and returned late in the
afternoon to cook dinner and experiment with the recipes
I had been shown. By the end of the year I was able to
prepare quite complicated dishes and to arrange a good
menu when special guests came to Monks House – that is,
when Mrs Woolf was well enough for friends to come and
see her.

Sometimes Mrs Woolf was quite ill while working on a
book and had acute headaches. Mr Woolf then had to
ration the number of friends who came to the house. Or,
to those who did come, he had to say that she would only
be able to talk to them for a short time. He did not like doing this but he knew that if she did not have enough rest
she would become very ill. Of course, her relations who
lived near by came to see her all the time – particularly
her sister Vanessa, and her niece Angelica. Mrs Woolf was
always delighted to see them. But, other than her relations, not many people who lived locally came to the
house at any time. When Mrs Woolf was well they
invited special friends to stay, most of them lived in London.

Of their friends, I particularly remember Kingsley
Martin. He came many times to Monks House and talked
a great deal about politics with Mr Woolf. Mrs Nicolson
[Vita Sackville-West] used to come over from Sissinghurst
and stay for the week-end. I liked her very much. She was
tall and beautiful, and had a rather rosy face. Mrs Woolf
was always so pleased when she came to see her. I particularly remember Mr Tom Eliot, too. He was a very gentle
person, quiet and reserved, but he talked a lot of the
time to Mrs Woolf and sometimes she used to tease him
and make him laugh. When he was staying for the week-
end I always hurried over from my cottage on a Sunday

morning to cook breakfast and then I would knock on Mr Eliot's door to let him know it was ready, only to find that he had gone to church and his room was empty. Mr and Mrs Woolf never went to church, and it was difficult to remember that he went every Sunday.

Another frequent visitor was Dame Ethel Smyth. She was very amusing: she used to drive over to Rodmell in her funny old car, get out and then stand at the gate shouting for Mrs Woolf. 'Virginia!' she would yell at the top of her voice. She was deaf and did not know how much noise she was making. Dame Ethel not only came many times to Monks House, she also wrote a letter to Mrs Woolf nearly every day. I used to collect the letters from the postman at my cottage in the morning – so that he would not wake Mr and Mrs Woolf too early – and Mrs Woolf always asked me if there was one from Dame Ethel, I think she looked forward to her letters. When Mr Woolf sat by her bed at breakfast-time to drink coffee and talk to her, she used to read the letter to him and it amused them very much.

Mrs Woolf was always delighted when she had finished writing a book, but the weeks following its completion were anxious ones for Mr Woolf. He knew that she might have some sort of nervous reaction to the long hours of hard work and so become ill again. If she began to develop bad headaches and look really exhausted, he stopped all visitors coming to the house and insisted that she had complete rest. I knew when Mrs Woolf's health was reaching this stage because she used to come into the kitchen and sit down and wonder what it was she had come to tell me. Then she would go out into the garden and walk about very slowly as though trying to remember. I have seen her bump into trees while she walked, not really knowing what she was doing. There were times, too, when she looked exhausted after they had driven down from London. I think this was usually in the winter when it was very cold. She hated to feel cold at any time: it seemed to affect her in a strange way – almost to frighten her. They used to sit by a log fire and drink coffee until she was warm and felt better.

I particularly remember Mrs Woolf coming to my cottage one afternoon. I was surprised to see her hurrying down the road, because she seldom came to see me, and I thought she must have something special to say. When she had sat down, she said, 'Louie, I have finished my book!' I knew then why she had come. She had been working for a long time on her novel *The Years*, and had been ill several times while trying to complete it. She was so delighted it was finished that she just had to come and tell someone. Then she said, 'Now we are going to spend some money and have the kitchen painted and a lot of new things put in for you.' She was so excited that we spent the rest of the afternoon making plans for the kitchen.

In spite of the exhaustion that Mrs Woolf suffered while writing her books, I always felt that she must be quite strong physically. Even when she had been very ill – as she was during the last few months of writing *The Years* – she managed to recover after a long rest. She was impatient with being ill and, I think, showed great courage in her determination to be well as quickly as possible.

But early in 1941, after finishing her last novel, Mrs Woolf was ill once more, and this time she seemed to have great difficulty in recovering. Mr Woolf was so worried about her that he persuaded her to see a specialist in Brighton. This was something I had not known her do before. With the specialist's help and with the care Mr Woolf took in seeing that she had as much rest as possible, she began to recover a little. One morning, when I was tidying Mr Woolf's study, they both came into the room and Mr Woolf said, 'Louie, will you give Mrs Woolf a duster so that she can help you clean the room?' He had been talking to her in her bedroom during the morning because it seemed to be one of her bad days again, and he must have suggested that she might like to do something, perhaps help with the housework. I gave her a duster, but it seemed very strange. I had never known her want to do any housework with me before. After a while Mrs Woolf put the duster down and went away. I thought that probably she did not like cleaning the study and had decided to do something else.

Later in the morning I saw her come downstairs from the sitting-room and go out to her room in the garden. In a few minutes she returned to the house, put on her coat, took her walking-stick and went quickly up the garden to the top gate. She must have been writing a letter to Mr Woolf and to her sister when she was in the sitting-room, then left them on the little coffee table and rushed off like that so that we would not see her.

When I rang the bell at 1 o'clock to tell Mr Woolf that lunch was ready, he said he was going upstairs to hear the news on the radio and would only be a few minutes. The next moment he came running down the stairs to the kitchen calling me. 'Louie!' he said, 'I think something has happened to Mrs Woolf! I think she might have tried to kill herself! Which way did she go – did you see her leave the house?' 'She went through the top gate a little while ago,' I said. It was suddenly a terrible nightmare. We ran out into the garden and I went to find the gardener, in case he had seen Mrs Woolf return. Mr Woolf went to the top gate and ran down towards the river. The gardener had not seen Mrs Woolf, so he went as fast as he could to find the policeman on duty in the village. They both went down to the river to see if they could help Mr Woolf. He had found her walking-stick stuck in the mud by the bank, but there was no sign of Mrs Woolf. They looked for her for a long time but there was nothing to tell them where she was. Mr Woolf wondered if she had left her stick there to mislead them and had perhaps gone up to Shepherd's Cottage. This was one of her favourite walks and it was possible she had gone that way so that she could be alone, not knowing really what she was doing. I went with him to Shepherd's Cottage, but she was not there. We went back and looked for her along the water meadows, and the river bank, and the brooks, until it was night-time and we had to give up. There was nothing more that any of us could do.

Two weeks later a policeman came to the house to tell Mr Woolf that her body had been found. Some children walking by the river from Lewes had seen her body washed into the side against the bank. He said that there were heavy stones in the pockets of her jacket and she must have put them there and then walked straight down into the river. And that was terrible. It was the most terrible thing I have known.

Monks House was a sad place for a long time afterwards. I got into a nervous state – with the worry of not knowing what had happened to Mrs Woolf and then with the shock of her body being found. When I heard anyone walk round the house to knock on the door I thought they must be coming to tell me something else I did not want to hear. I could not have borne any more bad news at that time.

I stayed on at Monks House to look after Mr Woolf during all the years that he was alone. He was always extremely busy: working at the Hogarth Press in London, going to political meetings, writing his books and, of course, looking after his garden. He loved his garden. With the help of Percy Bartholomew, his first gardener, he had made it a most beautiful place, full of flowers and fruit and vegetables. Mr Woolf was so active, he almost ran everywhere as though he needed more hours in the day, and he worked hard all the time. He really could work.

He was also a very kind and thoughtful man. When I was ill a few years ago, and had to have an operation, he came every day to the hospital in Brighton to talk to me. Although I was always so pleased to see him, he was then well over eighty and I was afraid that the journey might be too much for him. But he said that the journey did not tire him at all, and continued to come every day to see me until I was well enough to return home.

I had been back at Rodmell only a few weeks, and was still recovering from the operation, when he suddenly became very ill himself. A neighbour came running to my cottage one morning to ask me the name of Mr Woolf's doctor: she said that the gardener had found Mr Woolf lying in an armchair in his sitting-room and that he appeared to be very ill. I tried to hurry over to Monks House but I was still weak and could not go very fast. When I reached the house there was an ambulance outside and the driver said to me, 'Now, Mrs Mayer, you will have to put some of Mr Woolf's clothes together so that we can take him to hospital.' I asked him who had sent for the ambulance and he told me that someone had rung from the village. 'Well,' I said, 'you are not going to take Mr Woolf to hospital. I know it would not be his wish.' The driver knew that I meant what I said and, when I told him that I was going to ring Mr Woolf's doctor, he drove the ambulance away. Then I rang the doctor and waited until he came.

A neighbour and I looked after Mr Woolf night and day for several months. He recovered a little, but his illness had affected his speech and this made him very miserable. He asked me one day if I could understand what he was saying all the time : I had always told him the truth so I had to tell him that I could not follow what he said sometimes. Although he much preferred to be independent, he knew then that he would have to rest and be looked after. Eventually we had to have the help of two nurses and then the time came when no drugs or special treatment could do anything for him. But I stayed with him every day until the end.

When Mr Woolf died my work at Monks House came to an end. I had been there for thirty-six years. They were very happy years, I had loved my work, and become very fond of Mr and Mrs Woolf. I was always glad I had noticed that advertisement in the local newspaper in Southease all that time ago, and had answered it.

Rose Macaulay

'SHE had animation; she had sensibility; she had elegance, beauty and wit.' Thus Jane Austen, doing her descriptive utmost, might have approved Virginia Woolf. And between the animation, the sensibility, the elegance, the beauty and the wit, the essential quality would have slyly slipped, to look out mockingly from the turn of a phrase in talk, a sudden chuckle, a ridiculous question, a flashing piece of analysis or flight.

What made Virginia Woolf the most enchanting company in the world? Animation? There are plenty of animated talkers. Sensibility? There are many sensitive receivers. Zest? Again, plenty of that. Sympathy? Imagination? Wit? Irony? Culture? Brain? One hesitates to say that there are ever plenty of these; but they are not infrequently to be met. Yet they somehow combined in Virginia Woolf to make a person so rare and so delightful that she is not to be met elsewhere at all, so that getting her 'Come and see me' on a postcard was like being sent a free ticket to some stimulating entertainment.

With her, conversation was a flashing, many-faceted stream, now running swiftly, now slowing into still pools that shimmered with a hundred changing lights, shades and reflections, wherein sudden coloured fishes continually darted and stirred, now flowing between deep banks, now chuckling over sharp pebbles. She was sometimes pleased ironically to pose as the recluse who watched life from a quiet, drab corner, inviting her friends to tell her their fine stories of the world, of the rich parties they had doubtless attended, of the whirl of society from which they had just stepped, into which they would, she assured them, step again on leaving her. 'I think of you,' she would tell an unsociable visitor, 'as going from party to party, spinning round in the social whirl, leading a gay, rich, worldly life. Now tell me what is happening in the *beau monde.*' The visitor, particularly if young or hero-worshipping, had perhaps hoped for a deep, cultured kind of conversation, about books, about art, about life, about Proust. He sometimes, but not always, got it. Had he (or she) written a book, he might, if lucky, get a verbal review of it, an analysis, appreciation and criticism that was worth more than any printed review. All this public reviewing by authors of one another's books, Virginia regarded as a mistake; she thought that little worth saying was said that way; her notion was that newspaper reviews should only be of the dead; living writers, she said, would do better to review each other by word of mouth and to each other's faces, charging (since authors must live) a fee for doing so. (The scheme, I believe, never achieved a financial basis.)

How recapture or convey talk? That throaty, deepish, wholly attractive voice, throwing out some irrelevant and negligent inquiry, starting some hare – 'Is this a great age?' or 'Can there be Grand Old Women of literature, or only Grand Old Men? I think I shall prepare to be the Grand Old Woman of English letters. Or would you like to be?' Or, 'All this rubbish about Bloomsbury . . . I don't feel Bloomsbury; do you feel Marylebone (or Chelsea, Kensington or Hampstead)?' Comments on people – 'One of my geese. Geese usually like me; I have quite a flock; there must be something goosey about me, I'm afraid.' Her ironic, amused slant on clever young writers, 'the smarties'; on a vehement, black-browed talker, 'What charcoal fumes he emits!'; on adolescent university communists, 'They have no culture, only politics. Quite different from us, who had no politics, only culture.' Her interest in scandal: 'Go on; this is enthralling. People keep telling me different bits of this story; I feel as if a buried statue were being dug up piece by piece.' Her appreciation of people, in all their comic and delightful absurdities, their motley coats, the beauty and grace of the young, the learning of the learned, the wit of the brilliant, the simplicities of the simple. Such appreciation, such flattering discernment and interest, were heady fumes to intoxicate newcomers, evoking in them too often more of response than was convenient or required.

To tell her anything was like launching a ship on the shifting waters of a river, which flashed back a hundred reflections, enlarging, beautifying, animating, rippling about the keel, filling the sails, bobbing the craft up and down on dancing waves, enlarging the small trip into some fantastic Odyssean voyage among islands of exotic flowers and amusing beasts and men.

Did anyone ever have a dull moment in her company? Did she ever have a dull moment herself? Tragic, yes, since she had imagination, sensibility, and fine-drawn nerves: but dull? Improbable, since life gave her what it did, and she gave what she did to life. Her mischievousness, her firm, gay and determined prejudices, her shaping and creating genius, her haunted and haunting imagination, her sensitiveness, her humour, her scholarly love and knowledge of the past, the fastidiously exquisite and many-coloured form in which she clothed her thought, made her mind a rich kingdom to herself, an excitement to her friends, her writing a spell to bind her readers.

Yes, 'she had animation, she had sensibility, she had elegance, beauty and wit'; and behind all these a rare and fine-spun greatness. Her going seemed symbolic of the end of an age. Was it, as she inquired, a great age? Possibly not. But it was, anyhow, an age in which such as she could live and breathe; and it may likely enough be the last of these for a long time.

Raymond Mortimer

(Adapted from an interview
in the BBC Television film
A Night's Darkness. A Day's Sail)

*Do you recall with any vividness your first meeting with
Virginia Woolf?*

The first meeting that I clearly remember was in the
summer of 1924 when I went to stay with Maynard
Keynes and his wife, Lydia Lopokova, the dancer. They'd
taken a house at Studland on the Dorset coast. Leonard
and Virginia were there, and George Rylands who was
then an undergraduate. The weather was wonderful, and
I was absolutely bowled over by their liveliness of mind.
The first of the Bloomsbury Group I made friends with
was Clive Bell. I'd met him with Aldous Huxley who was
my contemporary at Balliol. And then I made friends
gradually with all of them. But my first vivid memory of
Virginia Woolf is at Studland, walking on the Downs
between blazing gorse-bushes.

*And did you start going to parties both in Bloomsbury
in London and Rodmell in Sussex about that time?*

Yes, I remember parties at the Keynes's above all, and
visits to Clive and Vanessa Bell and Duncan Grant at
Charleston. I only stayed at Rodmell once. I moved about
1924 from Chelsea to Bloomsbury, a house at the corner of
Gordon Square. The Woolfs were in Tavistock Square,

and the Keynes's, the James Stracheys, and Clive Bell were in Gordon Square, and Arthur Waley also. I went to live there chiefly for that reason.

What do you remember most vividly, or struck you most forcibly, about Virginia's appearance?

Well, it was extreme refinement and something ascetic too. Almost like that of an abbess – in the seventeenth or eighteenth century perhaps. Oddly I felt the same about Mrs Sidney Webb. Virginia had very beautiful hands and gestures. And, of course, the features were very distinctive. Her clothes I don't remember very much. She was thin and they hung rather loosely, they were not noticeable. She didn't dress fashionably, or even picturesquely. Her clothes were just rather unnoticeable because one was so fascinated by her gestures, her face, and above all her talk. She was the most enchanting conversationalist I've ever known. Jean Cocteau was perhaps a more brilliant talker, but he would give a performance, whereas hers you felt were entirely spontaneous – she was just letting her imagination rip.

What sort of things do you remember would set off this extraordinary flight of fancy which she was famed for?

Her fancy got going very often on yourself, the person she was talking to. And she began imagining what your life was, and then gradually her novelist's imagination took charge and instead of going on asking you what you did, she began to build up the most extraordinary sort of inverted pyramid of what she imagined your life was. It was a form of teasing in a way. I had a little house in Paris then, and she would say, 'Oh yes, I see you there, you are with princesses in tiaras and ambassadors in cocked hats, who are crowding up your stairs to meet

Picasso and Matisse and Gide ...' and so on. It was all totally unreal. I didn't know any ambassadors, and Matisse and Picasso and Gide never came to see me. I went to see them. And then gradually her picture became quite wild with the glory and splendour of your life, as she pretended. She was really laughing at one the whole time. But I have seen innocent victims swallow the whole thing and go away with their heads in the air thinking what extraordinary and enviable lives they were leading.

What do you think of the general charges often made against Bloomsbury of exclusiveness, arrogance and malice? Would you say these were true?

They were arrogant, I think, and there was almost a dynastic feeling among the Stephen ladies, Vanessa Bell and Virginia, and all the Stracheys. They were very much born in the intellectual purple and keenly aware of it. Virginia would often talk even about one of her closest friends as poor old so-and-so. But I shouldn't describe them as exclusive. There were a lot of people they thought priggish or uncouth or, worst of all, boring – or philistines or humbugs, whom they couldn't bear and wouldn't have anything to do with. But they didn't exclude me. I was just a young reviewer from a perfectly philistine background. They were deliciously kind and welcoming and friendly to me, and to a number of other unimportant people. But I was never a member of the Bloomsbury Group. They were older than I was, and all the men had been at Cambridge and rather despised Oxford men like myself. They were far more stimulating than any group of people that I'd met before – or indeed have met since. People who are young and couldn't have met any of them are apt to think that they were sombre and solemn. But this was not so. They were serious, very, very serious, about art and ideas and personal relationships, but the general tone of talk was extremely light and they all loved fun. They were tremendously joky people, making cracks and teasing one another. They also laughed a lot about the sexual life of their friends, in a way that was thought shocking in that still unpermissive age.

Did you ever see the melancholy side of Virginia?

No, I can't say I ever noticed it, though I knew of its existence. She loved social life. And her husband had to ration this for her because she was easily exhausted. But one always got the impression that she was delighted to see one, or to see anyone. It cheered her up, it unleashed her imagination.

Do you think Virginia Woolf was a genius?

A genius. Well, I do – yes, I should say she was a genius, not evidently of the highest order. But a delicate genius, I think, above all in her use of words. In her best writings, in *The Waves* and *Mrs Dalloway* and *To the Lighthouse* and in all her essays – *The Common Reader* and the others – the words are all alive, they're like a shoal of fish jumping in a net. There is nothing dead at all about her language. And she took enormous trouble. She would write a review eight or nine times over, and the result is that you do get this feeling of lightness and spontaneity. Never a cliché, nothing heavy.

Were you aware of her genius when you were with her?

Much more so than with some of the other writers who I think had genius, notably Ivy Compton-Burnett. And I think her best writing is very like what her talk was, but of course more disciplined. I don't think she was one of the supreme novelists. She failed to put herself into the shoes of people very different from herself. Balzac and Tolstoy seem to have known exactly, Proust also largely, what any coarse, money-minded or brutal human being was like – well, I don't think Virginia did. She had too fine a temperament to understand human beastliness and human vulgarity. In a way her own fineness of character, I think, limited her powers of characterization. The same is true of Jane Austen (though she was a supreme novelist), but not of Balzac and Tolstoy and Proust, who all had pretty horrible sides to their characters. But Virginia, I think, had very little that was horrid in her character. She was consumed with certain neurotic jealousies of other writers, of people she need never have bothered about because they weren't in her class at all, but that was part of her neurosis. She wasn't money-minded or in any way coarse.

Surely rather malicious though?

Yes, I should say she was malicious.

She could wound people deeply?

Seldom, I believe. I saw her teasing people but never actually hurting anyone, though her letters to Lytton Strachey do reveal a horrid streak of malice.

Madge Garland

In the twenties, when I was Fashion Editor of *Vogue* Magazine, many members of the Bloomsbury Group wrote articles for *Vogue*'s editorial departments – art, literature, architecture, the theatre. Their work was commissioned by Dorothy Todd – Dody, as she was known to her friends – a brilliantly perceptive editor, whose aim was to make *Vogue* into a magazine of such literary and social importance that it would be acceptable everywhere. It was during these years, the time when these articles were being commissioned, that I came to know Virginia Woolf.

I had first seen her – though at the time I did not know who she was – at an art lecture given by Roger Fry in London. I was very young and did not know anybody at the lecture, but I saw a very beautiful woman sitting in the audience: she had an angular face, high cheek-bones, deep-set eyes, an almost madonna-like appearance. There was a presence about her that made her instantly noticeable. But what also attracted my attention was that she appeared to be wearing an upturned wastepaper basket on her head. There sat this beautiful and distinguished woman wearing what could only be described as a wastepaper basket.

Some years later, when I knew Virginia, I discovered

that she did not have the time, or even the wish, to find clothes that suited her. But she was interested in them and conscious of their importance. Fortunately for me, I had the opportunity of choosing an entire outfit for her, and so was able to put all that beauty into its right setting. This occurred early in 1925 when Virginia's collection of essays, *The Common Reader*, had been published and had been followed closely by the publication of her fourth novel, *Mrs Dalloway*. These two books had been praised by the critics and Virginia had become even more of a literary figure than she already was. Her circle of friends had widened, too, and she was beginning to lead – perhaps against her wishes – a fuller social life. She asked me to choose clothes that would be suitable for her to wear at special dinner parties and to the theatre.

I was delighted to do this and went to see my friend Nicole Groult, the Parisian dressmaker and younger sister of Paul Poiret, the brilliant dress designer. I ordered a long silk coat and dress, which Nicole designed and had made in her Paris *salon*. When it arrived it was absolutely beautiful. Alas I cannot remember the colour of this lovely outfit now, but Virginia looked supremely elegant in it and was so pleased and happy because its creation had not taken a moment of her time. When Nicole came over to show her collection in London she brought a fitter with her and they saw the coat and dress on Virginia in case there were any last-minute adjustments to be made. At this fitting Virginia said to me, 'If only you would always dress me I should have time to write an extra book which I would dedicate to you!' I wish this had been possible. A book dedicated to me by Virginia would have given me immense pleasure.

Virginia wrote an occasional article for *Vogue* and she, Dody Todd and I sometimes lunched together when they were in the process of being commissioned. We found that once her initial shyness was overcome she could be an enchanting and extraordinarily amusing person. In those early days many of her friends – most of them members of the Bloomsbury Group – were also writing for *Vogue* : I particularly remember articles by Lytton Strachey and Roger Fry. Aldous Huxley was on our editorial staff; he wrote theatre and book reviews. His work was taken over by a very young Raymond Mortimer. Clive Bell was our art critic. I also remember Edith Sitwell writing for us – although she, of course, was not a member of the Bloomsbury Group.

Dody Todd soon made *Vogue* the most highbrow magazine of its kind; a concept no longer applicable to – or even desirable for – fashion magazines today. She had an extraordinary gift for making people feel that they, and only they, could write about a particular subject. She had the ability to approach the right person in the right way and managed to persuade most of the literary figures of the day to contribute. As well as articles of literary importance, *Vogue* contained photographs of the authors, of their houses and of their friends. It published one of the most successful pictures of Virginia; I arranged for this to be taken by that now forgotten photographic team, Beck and Macgregor, and went to their studio to greet her there. She refers to this incident in her diary.

The luncheon parties involved with commissioning the articles always provided the most pleasant part of our day. Dody studied the likes and dislikes of her guests very carefully; she remembered that Virginia hated going into restaurants and much preferred to have lunch in a house or flat with people whom she knew. While thinking how best to overcome this unusual situation, she mentioned Virginia's dislike of restaurants to a friend of hers, Marcel

Boulestin. At this time Marcel was music critic for the
French newspaper *Le Temps*; he had a flat in Southampton Row, where he cooked his favourite French dishes in
his own kitchen. He disliked English food – saying it was
badly cooked and so dull.

When Marcel heard about Virginia's antipathy towards restaurants he suggested he should arrange the
whole meal and that the luncheon party should be held
in his flat. It was a marvellous idea. Dody knew that the
food would be superb and the surroundings suitable to
the occasion. In the end, Marcel produced some splendid
dishes and his friend Robin Adair waited on us. Alan
Walton, who was a well-known and talented artist, and
the novelist Leo Myers were there too. The party was a
great success and Virginia enjoyed herself enormously.

After this happy luncheon party we said to Marcel that
it would be wonderful if he owned a small restaurant to
which all of us could go just to meet and enjoy meals arranged by him. And this is what happened. Leo Myers,
who was rich, put up the money, Marcel took over some
small premises in Leicester Square, and Alan Walton did
the decorations. It was just for French food and was so
small that it was really like a club; we never went there
without knowing everyone, which was one of its great
charms. And so it was partly owing to Virginia and her
dislike of restaurants that Marcel started his own unique
restaurant, Boulestin's, which was to become so famous
in later years.

There is one other anecdote that I remember in connection with Virginia. Again it was at a luncheon party.
Virginia wanted to meet a friend of mine, Sylvia Townsend Warner, so I invited them both to lunch at my
home in Chelsea. Sylvia's novel about ghosts, witches and
warlocks, *Lolly Willowes*, had just been published and I

thought that it would probably provide an interesting topic of conversation. As I think most people know, Virginia always greeted anyone she did not know well with a barrage of questions. She fired several at Sylvia and then asked, 'How is it that you know so much about witches?' To which Sylvia replied, 'Because I am one!' For a moment I thought that my arrangement for them to meet had been a ghastly mistake, but Virginia, having looked rather disconcerted for a second, suddenly laughed – one of her characteristic hoots of laughter – and the awkward situation was overcome as quickly as it had arrived.

Virginia could be a very enchanting person, as she proved to be on this occasion with Sylvia, but there were times when I felt that this was the wrong definition for her and that she was more nearly *enchanted*. This was when she seemed removed from the people she was talking to – almost dreamlike. In those days I did not know about her mental illnesses : they were not obvious to me. But I think that this strange impression she sometimes gave of being enchanted was in some way connected with them, although I am not certain if I am right. But there is one thing I am sure about – I wish that Virginia had been able to write that extra book and dedicate it to me.

Christopher Isherwood

DURING March 1941 I was working at Metro-Goldwyn-Mayer studios on the screenplay of a film. One day, one of the movie-columnists, who used to rove around the studios picking up bits of information, dropped into my office and asked if he might use my phone. He wanted to call his own office and find out if any messages had come in for him. I told him to go ahead and turned back to my work, listening with half an ear to him talking to his assistant: 'No – *no*, you dope – the name's Woolf – W-O-O-L F – sure, I'm sure – sure, I've heard of her, you ignorant bastard – she was a great writer – British...'

That was how I learned of Virginia Woolf's death.

Klaus Mann asked me to write about her for *Decision*, a magazine which he had just started. This piece appeared in the May number of 1941. I exhume it for the sake of some descriptive passages which do seem to me to evoke Virginia Woolf as I knew her. But, of all my exhibits, this is the one I have been most tempted to tamper with. An attempt to speak simultaneously as the public eulogist and the private mourner is almost foredoomed to falseness; all the more so when you feel you are addressing strangers who could never really understand or care. One sentence in particular nauseates me as much as anything I have ever written: 'she was, as the Spaniards say, "very rare" . . .' This bit of jargon was undoubtedly inspired by Hemingway's *For Whom the Bell Tolls*, which I had recently read and reviewed enthusiastically (I now admire it less than his other novels). But it would be cowardly to blame Hemingway. To ape the affectations of great writers is never excusable.

I did seriously consider cutting the sentence out of this reprint. Then I remembered that the piece has already appeared in a college textbook which is designed to teach Form and Style in writing modern prose. So let my lapse be recorded here also, as a warning to the young!

The 'Jeremy' referred to is a pseudonym for Hugh Walpole. Virginia teased him endlessly but was very fond of him, I believe. He took her teasing with good humour, feeling humble and honoured to be in her presence. He seems to have been a generous, warm-natured, thoroughly sympathetic person. I wish I had known him better.

*

Virginia Woolf is dead – and thousands of people, far outside the immediate circle of her friends and colleagues, will be sorry, will feel the loss of a great and original talent to our literature. For she was famous, surprisingly famous when one considers that she was what is called 'a writer's writer'. Her genius was intensely feminine and personal – private, almost. To read one of her books was (if you liked it) to receive a letter from her, addressed specially to you. But this, perhaps, was just the secret of her appeal.

As everybody knows, Mrs Woolf was a prominent member of what journalists used to call 'The Bloomsbury Group' – which includes Lytton Strachey, Vanessa Bell, Duncan Grant, E. M. Forster, Arthur Waley, Desmond MacCarthy and Maynard Keynes. Actually, the 'Group' was not a group at all, in the self-conscious sense, but a kind of clan; one of those 'natural' families which form themselves without the assistance of parents, uncles and aunts, simply because a few sensitive and imaginative people become aware of belonging to each other, and wish to be frequently in each other's company. It follows, of course, that these brothers and sisters under the skin find it convenient to settle in the same neighbourhood – Bloomsbury, in this case. It is a district just behind and beyond the British Museum. Its three large squares, Gordon, Bedford and Tavistock, have something of the dignity and atmosphere of Cambridge college courts.

Open *To the Lighthouse*, *The Common Reader* or *The Waves*, read a couple of pages with appreciation, and you have become already a distant relative of the Bloomsbury Family. You can enter the inner sanctum, the Woolf drawing-room, and nobody will rise to greet you – for you are one of the party. 'Oh, come in,' says Virginia, with that gracious informality which is so inimitably aristocratic, 'you know everybody, don't you? We were just talking about Charles Tansley ... poor Charles – such a prig... Imagine what he said the other day...' And so, scarcely aware, we float into our story.

The Bloomsbury Family held together by consanguinity of talent. That you could express yourself artistically, through the medium of writing or painting or music, was taken for granted. This was the real business of life: it would have been indecent, almost, to refer to it. Artistic integrity was the family religion; and in its best days it could proudly boast that it did not harbour a single prostitute, pot-boiler or hack. Nevertheless one must live. Some of the brothers and sisters had very odd hobbies. Keynes, for example, whose brilliant descriptive pen could touch in an unforgettable and merciless portrait of

Clemenceau on the margin, as it were, of an economic report to the Versailles treaty-makers – Keynes actually descended into that sordid jungle, the City, and emerged a wealthy man! And Virginia – the exquisite, cloistered Virginia – became a publisher. True, the thing happened by gradual stages. It began as a sort of William Morris handicraft – with Leonard and Virginia working their own press, and Virginia's delicate fingers, one supposes, getting black with printer's ink. But all this was ancient history, and the hand-press was stowed away in the cellar under dust-sheets before the day in the early thirties when I first walked timidly up the steps of the house in Tavistock Square.

It is usually easy to describe strangers. Yet, although I didn't meet Virginia more than half a dozen times, I find it nearly impossible to write anything about her which will carry the breath of life. Which century did she belong to? Which generation? You could not tell: she simply defied analysis. At the time of our first meeting, she was, I now realize, an elderly lady, yet she seemed, in some mysterious way, to be very much older and very much younger than her age. I could never decide whether she reminded me of my grandmother as a young Victorian girl, or my great-grandmother – if she had taken some rejuvenating drug and lived a hundred and twenty years, to become the brilliant leader of an intensely modern Georgian *salon*.

One remembers, first of all, those wonderful, forlorn eyes; the slim, erect, high-shouldered figure, strangely tense, as if always on the alert for some distant sound; the hair folded back from the eggshell fragility of the temples; the small, beautifully cut face, like a Tenny-sonian cameo – Mariana, or The Lady of Shalott. Yes, that is the impression one would like to convey – an

unhappy, high-born lady in a ballad, a fairy-story princess under a spell; slightly remote from the rest of us, a
profile seen against the dying light, hands dropped help-
lessly in the lap, a shocking, momentary glimpse of intense grief.

What rubbish! We are at the tea table. Virginia is
sparkling with gaiety, delicate malice and gossip – the
gossip which is the style of her books and which made her
the best hostess in London; listening to her, we missed
appointments, forgot love-affairs, stayed on and on into
the small hours, when we had to be hinted, gently, but
firmly, out of the house. This time the guest of honour is
a famous novelist, whose substantial income proves that
Art, after all, can really pay. He is modest enough – but
Virginia, with sadistic curiosity, which is like the teasing
of an elder sister, drags it all out of him : how much time
New York publishers gave, how much the movie people,
and what the King said, and the Crown Prince of Sweden
– she has no mercy. And then, when it is all over, 'You
know, Jeremy,' she tells him, smiling almost tenderly,
'you remind me of a very beautiful prize-winning cow ...'
'A cow, Virginia ...?' The novelist gulps but grins bravely
at me; determined to show he can take it. 'Yes ... a very,
very fine cow. You go out into the world, and win all sorts
of prizes, but gradually your coat gets covered with burs,
and so you have to come back again into your field. And
in the middle of the field is a rough old stone post, and
you rub yourself against it to get the burs off. Don't you
think, Leonard ...' she looks across at her husband, 'that
that's our real mission in life? We're Jeremy's old stone
scratching-post.'

What else is there to say about her? Critics will place
her among the four greatest English women writers.
Friends will remember her beauty, her uniqueness, her

charm. I am very proud to have known her. Was she the bewitched princess, or the wicked little girl at the tea party – or both, or neither? I can't tell. In any case she was, as the Spaniards say, 'very rare', and this world was no place for her. I am happy to think that she is free of it, before everything she loved has been quite smashed. If I wanted an epitaph for her, taken from her own writings, I should choose this:

It was done; it was finished. Yes, she thought, laying down her brush in extreme fatigue, I have had my vision.

Stephen Spender

SINCE I occasionally 'teach' Virginia Woolf to students, I find it impossible to write about her without their attitude taking up a position in the foreground of my mind which tends to interrupt memories and impressions of her. I should say that on the whole she 'means' rather little to students today. To some students, particularly Americans, she represents a good deal that they dislike about English writing. At the University of Connecticut, where I took a modern literature course, I asked my students to read *The Waves*. When I next met them, the young man whom I had asked to start off the seminar began: 'I attribute the cold I have been suffering from all the week to my having to read and prepare to talk about *The Waves*.'

This attitude is characteristic of a good many students today. Virginia Woolf simply means nothing to them. To them it seems that her fiction records a very limited and very English society, seen through the eyes and minds of a few slightly drawn characters of extremely attenuated sensibility who regard the world of action, in so far as it impinges on them at all (as it does, for example, in the rather two-dimensional character of Percival in *The Waves*), from a very great distance, as though through the wrong end of a telescope. Healthy sensual appetites also scarcely touch on this world. As for Virginia Woolf's writing, such students regard it as imagistic, poetic and hardly worth unravelling, because they are sure that it will not provide a thread that will lead them to some significant piece of action or characterization, or some total view of reality, which they expect of a novel.

The few students who do like Virginia Woolf (they are usually girls) do so partly because they regard her as a feminist, partly because her novels offer them the prospect of enigmas, strange symbolic patterns, by which they can become mystified, as by James's *The Figure in the Carpet*.

I find it difficult to deal with either of these attitudes. Virginia Woolf is certainly 'caviare to the general'. And to those like my student with the cold to whom she means nothing, it is probably best to say nothing. But it is equally difficult to discuss her with those who smile with secret superior satisfaction when she is mentioned. It is not, however, my business to discuss her writing in recording a few impressions of her. But since the value of recollections is based on the presumed gold of her work, I should attempt to convey, as briefly as possible, the reasons why I attach importance to it.

Imaginatively, she is I think the inhabitant of two worlds. One of these is the isolated self, her own sensibility of which she is almost the prisoner, and of which the various female characters who are the heroines of her novels – Mrs Dalloway, Mrs Ramsay, Orlando – are but masks. This self is Adam-like – or, since she is a woman, should I say Eve-like? Her approach to the outer world is that she is completely isolated, and unique, and that every instant – the sun shining on the leaves, the bird singing from the branches – is unprecedented, unique, and will never happen again. It has happened, like the Creation, for the first time.

One can well understand that this attitude is very irritating to many people. It is based, of course, on a literal truth about experience – every event and every pair of eyes staring at it is unique – but it is a truism which, for the purposes of living, most people ignore: just as they ignore another truth about the human situation – that at any moment the world might come to an end through some object from outer space colliding with it. An artist whose vision of life was based on the perpetual contingency of an immanent catastrophe, which in several million years has not occurred, would probably irritate his readers. Virginia Woolf's view of life as consisting of confrontations between beings and objects totally separate is, of course, more valid than this – in fact it is true enough of what many people feel to be disturbing. Nevertheless, on the whole, people's lives are based on ignoring both their own loneliness and the uniqueness and unprecedentedness of each moment in time that carries on it the burden of consciousness of the universe.

The view opposite to Virginia Woolf's compulsive vision – from which she could not, I am sure, ever escape for a moment – is that life is a routine. The routine view of life is that it consists of lots of precedents which have consequences. Precedents and consequences form chains of behaviour, and to live you have to relate your own life to these tracks of connections – as you also have to do to understand other people, to understand history, to understand anything about behaviour at all. Everything that is achieved in the world is achieved as the result of a routine: not just the routine itself – going to the office every morning – but a vision of life as routine. The routine vision extends far beyond time-tables and offices, it extends to one's ideas about the characters and behaviour of other people. The characters in novels, for example, are for the most part hitched on to going to school, falling in love, getting married – behaving in ways which show that according to established routines they are villains or heroes, or something a bit subtler between the two, or that makes them both at the same time.

Virginia Woolf was aware of course of routines. But they seemed to her strange. She stood outside them. They were also particularly associated in her mind with the male sex. The man, rather than the woman, was a creature of routine. The more he excelled at it the more absurd he appeared in Virginia Woolf's eye; so that a highly successful man who became Prime Minister, or an admiral, was like a creature with bright golden chains not only hung on him but visibly running all through him. Some women in Virginia Woolf's world were outside routines. They saw the world as a moment to moment flashing on of physical and mental events which never ceased to surprise, never lost their wonder. In order to please their men these women pretended to accept the routine view of life; but they never really did so, and the fact that they had to play this game with their husbands, of pretending to believe, made men faintly absurd and certainly opaque.

The second world which Virginia Woolf belonged to was the group – or, to put it less kindly, the clique. As Leonard Woolf's autobiography shows, she moved in a very limited social world consisting of herself, her sister Vanessa and her brother Thoby, her husband, and a few friends – among them, notably, Lytton Strachey, Maynard Keynes, Roger Fry and Duncan Grant. This was the group called Bloomsbury. She tended to regard anyone outside these friends as a two-dimensional figure. I can well remember seeing Hugh Walpole in Virginia

Woolf's drawing-room. In her presence (he adored her and relished with the richest masochism what was happening to him) he turned into a papier-mâché mask in a carnival: rubicund, beaming, bobbing his head up and down in agreement with her, and producing answers to her teasing questions which showed that inside he was also made of a kind of spiritual papier-mâché. The inquisition was kept strictly on the material level, as befitted his best-selling status. 'How many copies of your next book do you expect to sell, Hugh?' 'Two hundred thousand, Virginia.' She elicited the information from him that a warehouse was at this moment being stacked with paper for printing the new best-seller. 'How exciting. Then you will be able to buy a gold-plated car?' She teased Hugh with the fact that his chauffeur looked *exactly* like him: they were indistinguishable, she said.

I should mention that Virginia Woolf objected to the name 'Bloomsbury'. After I had published a book in which I discussed Bloomsbury, she told me rather sharply that if I insisted on referring to her as belonging to Bloomsbury she would refer to me and to my neighbour William Plomer as 'Maida Vale'. We both lived in that part of London at the time. I do not mean to insist on the 'Bloomsbury', then. It is much more important to say that her second world was an inner world in which her family and her friends played roles in her imagination: in which they existed, as I say, as a group, revering one another, believing in the talents of each and all, exchanging ideas, gossip and confidences. Each member of the group was a part of a shared consciousness. There was interaction between her isolation and her sense of friendship which gave the group the character of a work of art of relations achieved and of values intensely imagined. Communication between them was ideal, together with the wit, the story-telling, the malice, the gossip and the entertainment – only very thin walls dividing the rooms where they met from tragedy. If there was tragedy, they could talk about it.

The Waves is a prose poem about the group of friends whose lives, from birth almost, play to one another like the instruments in quartet or quintet. Yet each member of the group has projected upon him or her Virginia Woolf's sense of isolation. It is both a real harmony between inter-related lives and a multi-faced mask of human loneliness. It seems to me a book of great beauty and a prose poem of genius. Having said this I am brought up against the blank wall of so many readers' total lack of sympathy for it. An objection I have frequently heard is that in the opening pages – which for a work with 'musical' themes and instrumentation are certainly of great importance – the 'voices' of the children Bernard, Susan, Rhoda, Neville, Jinny and Louis are not distinguishable. To me, they seem completely distinct, and I could certainly demonstrate this by drawing attention to the symbols attached to each character which distinguish them. However, rationalizing the text, though I suppose it might enable one to win a classroom argument, scarcely seems relevant here. One is either convinced by a poetry which seems as beautiful to me – dare I say it – as *Les Illuminations*, or one has eyes that do not see, ears that do not hear. Despite Bloomsbury's irreligion – which Virginia Woolf loyally shared – *The Waves* is essentially a religious or mystical work, a poem about vision, prayer, poetry itself, the open and aware attention which people can pay to one another within the context of shared values and circumstances, throughout life.

The extraordinary concentration of this book is surely due to the fact that it was only through her intense and creative imagining of a group of friends who watched and marvelled at one another, separated but always came back together, that Virginia Woolf could escape sometimes from the total isolation – madness – of the first world.

E. M. Forster

As soon as we dismiss the legend of the Invalid Lady of Bloomsbury, so guilelessly accepted by Arnold Bennett, we find ourselves in a bewildering world where there are few headlines. We think of *The Waves* and say 'Yes – that is Virginia Woolf': then we think of *The Common Reader*, where she is different, of *A Room of One's Own* or of the preface to *Life as We Have Known It*: different again. She is like a plant which is supposed to grow in a well-prepared garden bed – the bed of esoteric literature – and then pushes up suckers all over the place, through the gravel of the front drive, and even through the flag-stones of the kitchen yard. She was full of interests, and their number increased as she grew older, she was curious about life, and she was tough, sensitive but tough.

There is, after all, one little lifeline to catch hold of: she liked writing.

These words, which usually mean so little, must be applied to her with all possible intensity. She liked receiving sensations – sights, sounds, tastes – passing them through her mind, where they encountered theories and memories, and then bringing them out again, through a pen, on to a bit of paper. Now began the higher delights of authorship. For these pen-marks on paper were only the prelude to writing, little more than marks on a wall. They had to be combined, arranged, emphasized here, eliminated there, new relationships had to be generated, new penmarks born, until out of the interactions, something, one thing, one, arose. This one thing, whether it was a novel or an essay or a short story or a biography or a private paper to be read to her friends, was, if it was so successful, itself analogous to a sensation. Although it was so complex and intellectual, although it might be large and heavy with facts, it was akin to the very simple things which had started it off, to the sights, sounds, tastes. It could be best described as we describe them. For it was not about something. It was something. This is obvious in 'aesthetic' works, like *Kew Gardens* and *Mrs Dalloway*; it is less obvious in a work of learning, like the *Roger Fry*, yet here too the analogy holds. We know, from an article by R. C. Trevelyan, that she had, when writing it, a notion corresponding to the notion of a musical composition. In the first chapter she stated the themes, in the subsequent chapters she developed them separately, and she tried to bring them all in again at the end. The biography is duly about Fry. But it is something else too; it is one thing, one.

She liked writing with an intensity which few writers have attained or even desired. Most of them write with half an eye on their royalties, half an eye on their critics, and a third half eye on improving the world, which leaves them with only half an eye for the task on which she concentrated her entire vision. She would not look elsewhere, and her circumstances combined with her temperament to focus her. Money she had not to consider, because she possessed a private income, and though financial independence is not always a safeguard against commercialism, it was in her case. Critics she never considered while she was writing, although she could be attentive to them and even humble afterwards. Improving the world she would not consider, on the ground that the world is man-made, and that she, a woman, had no responsibility for the mess. This last opinion is a curious one, and I shall be returning to it; still, she held it, it completed the circle of her defences, and neither the desire for money nor the desire for reputation nor philanthropy could influence her. She had a singleness of purpose which will not recur in this country for many years, and writers who have liked writing as she liked it have not indeed been common in any age.

Now the pitfall for such an author is obvious. It is the Palace of Art, it is that bottomless chasm of dullness which pretends to be a palace, all glorious with corridors and domes, but which is really a dreadful hole into which the unwary aesthete may tumble, to be seen no more. She has all the aesthete's characteristics: selects and manipulates her impressions; is not a great creator of character; enforces patterns on her books; has no great cause at heart. So how did she avoid her appropriate pitfall and remain up in the fresh air, where we can hear the sound of the stable-boy's boots, or boats bumping, or Big Ben; where we can taste really new bread, and touch real dahlias?

She had a sense of humour, no doubt, but our answer must go a little deeper than that hoary nostrum. She escaped, I think, because she liked writing for fun. Her pen amused her, and in the midst of writing seriously this other delight would spurt through. A little essay called *On Being Ill*, exemplifies this. It starts with the thesis that illness in literature is seldom handled properly (De Quincey and Proust were exceptional), that the body is treated by novelists as if it were a sheet of glass through which the soul gazes, and that it is contrary to experience. There are possibilities in the thesis, but she soon wearies of exploring them. Off she goes amusing herself, and after half a dozen pages she is writing entirely for fun, caricaturing the type of people who visit sick-rooms, insisting that Augustus Hare's *Two Noble Lives* is the book an invalid most demands, and so on. She could describe illness if she chose – for instance, in *The Voyage Out* – but she gaily forgets it in *On Being Ill*. The essay is slight, still it does neatly illustrate the habit of her mind. Literature was her merry-go-round as well as her study. This makes her amusing to read, and it also saves her from the Palace of Art. For you cannot enter the Palace of Art, therein to dwell, if you are tempted from time to time to play the fool. Lord Tennyson did not consider that. His remedy, you remember, was that the Palace would be purified when it was inhabited by all mankind, all behaving seriously at once. Virginia Woolf found a simpler and a sounder solution.

No doubt there is a danger here – there is danger everywhere. She might have become a glorified *diseuse*, who frittered away her broader effects by mischievousness, and she did give that impression to some who met her in the flesh; there were moments when she could scarcely see the busts for the moustaches she pencilled on them, and when the bust was a modern one, whether of a gentleman in a top hat or of a youth on a pylon, it had no chance of remaining sublime. But in her writing, even in her light writing, central control entered. She was master of her complicated equipment, and though most of us like to write sometimes seriously and sometimes in fun, few of us can so manage the two impulses that they speed each other up, as hers did.

The above remarks are more or less introductory. It seems convenient now to recall what she did write, and to say a little about her development. She began back in 1915 with *The Voyage Out* – a strange, tragic, inspired novel about English tourists in an impossible South American hotel; her passion for truth is here already, mainly in the form of atheism, and her passion for wisdom is here in the form of music. The book made a deep impression upon the few people who read it. Its successor, *Night and Day*, disappointed them. This is an exercise in classical realism, and contains all that has characterized English fiction, for good and evil, during the last two hundred years : faith in personal relations, recourse to humorous side-shows, geographical exactitude, insistence on petty social differences : indeed most of the devices she so gaily derides in *Mr Bennett and Mrs Brown*. The style has been normalized and dulled. But at the same time she published two short stories, *Kew Gardens*, and *The Mark on the Wall*. These are neither dull nor normal; lovely little things; her style trails after her as she walks and talks, catching up dust and grass in its folds, and instead of the precision of the earlier writings we have something more elusive than had yet been achieved in English. Lovely little things, but they seemed to lead nowhere, they were all tiny dots and coloured blobs, they were an inspired breathlessness, they were a beautiful droning or gasping which trusted to luck. They were perfect as far as they went, but that was not far, and none of us guessed that out of the pollen of those flowers would come the trees of the future. Consequently when *Jacob's Room* appeared in 1922 we were tremendously surprised. The style and sensitiveness of *Kew Gardens* remained, but they were applied to human relationships, and to the structure of society. The blobs of colour continue to drift past, but in their midst, interpreting their course like a closely sealed jar, stands the solid figure of a young man. The improbable has occurred; a method essentially poetic and apparently trifling has been applied to fiction. She was still uncertain of the possibilities of the new technique, and *Jacob's Room* is an uneven little book, but it represents her great departure, and her abandonment of the false start of *Night and Day*. It leads on to her genius in its fullness; to *Mrs Dalloway* (1925), *To the Lighthouse* (1927), and *The Waves* (1931). These successful works are all suffused with poetry and enclosed in it. *Mrs Dalloway* has the framework of a London summer's day, down which go spiralling two fates: the fate of the sensitive worldly hostess, and the fate of the sensitive obscure maniac; though they never touch they are closely connected, and at the same moment we lose sight of them both. It is a civilized book, and it was written from personal experience. In her work, as in her private problems, she was always civilized and sane on the subject of madness. She pared the edges off this particular malady, she tied it down to being a malady, and robbed it of the evil magic it has acquired through timid or careless thinking; here is one of the gifts we have to thank her for. *To the Lighthouse* is, however, a much greater achievement, partly because the chief characters in it, Mr and Mrs Ramsay, are so interesting. They hold us, we think of them away from their surroundings, and yet they are in accord with those surroundings, with the poetic scheme. *To the Lighthouse* is in three movements. It has been called a novel in sonata form, and certainly the slow central section, conveying the passing of time, does demand a musical analogy. We have, when reading it, the rare pleasure of inhabiting two worlds at once, a pleasure only art can give: the world where a little boy wants to go to a lighthouse but never manages it until, with changed emotions, he goes there as a young man; and the world where there is pattern, and this world is emphasized by passing much of the observation through the mind of Lily Briscoe, who is a painter. Then comes

The Waves. Pattern here is supreme – indeed it is italicized. And between the motions of the sun and the waters, which preface each section, stretch, without interruption, conversation, words in inverted commas. It is a strange conversation, for the six characters, Bernard, Neville, Louis, Susan, Jinny, Rhoda, seldom address one another, and it is even possible to regard them (like Mrs Dalloway and Septimus) as different facets of one single person. Yet they do not conduct internal monologues, they are in touch amongst themselves, and they all touch the character who never speaks, Percival. At the end, most perfectly balancing their scheme, Bernard, the would-be novelist, sums up, and the pattern fades out. *The Waves* is an extraordinary achievement, an immense extension of the possibilities of *Kew Gardens* and *Jacob's Room*. It is trembling on the edge. A little less – and it would lose its poetry. A little more – and it would be over into the abyss, and be dull and arty. It is her greatest book, though *To the Lighthouse* is my favourite.

It was followed by *The Years*. This is another experiment in the realistic tradition. It chronicles the fortunes of a family through a documented period. As in *Night and Day*, she deserts poetry, and again she fails. But in her posthumous novel *Between the Acts* she returns to the method she understood. Its theme is a village pageant, which presents the entire history of England, and into which, at the close, the audience is itself drawn, to continue that history: 'The curtain rose' is its concluding phrase. The conception is poetic, and the text of the pageant is mostly written in verse. She loved her country – her country that is the 'country', and emerges from the unfathomable past. She takes us back in this exquisite final tribute, and she points us on, and she shows us through her poetic vagueness something more solid than patriotic history, and something better worth dying for.

Amongst all this fiction, nourishing it and nourished by it, grow other works. Two volumes of *The Common Reader* show the breadth of her knowledge and the depth of her literary sympathy; let anyone who thinks her an exquisite recluse read what she says on Jack Mytton the foxhunter. As a critic she could enter into anything – anything lodged in the past, that is to say; with her contemporaries she sometimes had difficulties. Then there are the biographies, fanciful and actual. *Orlando* is, I need hardly say, an original book, and the first part of it is splendidly written : the description of the Great Frost is already received as a 'passage' in English literature, whatever a passage may be. After the transformation of sex things do not go so well; the authoress seems unconvinced by her own magic and somewhat fatigued by it, and the biography finishes competently rather than brilliantly; it has been a fancy on too large a scale, and we can see her getting bored. But *Flush* is a complete success, and exactly what it sets out to be; the material, the method, the length, accord perfectly, it is doggie without being silly, and it does give us, from the altitude of the carpet or the sofa-foot, a peep at high poetic personages, and a new angle on their ways. The biography of Roger Fry – one should not proceed direct from a spaniel to a Slade Professor, but Fry would not have minded and spaniels mind nothing – reveals a new aspect of her powers, the power to suppress herself. She indulges in a pattern, but she never intrudes her personality or over-handles her English; respect for her subject dominates her, and only occasionally – as in her description of the divinely ordered chaos of Fry's studio with its still-life of apples and eggs labelled 'please do not touch' – does she allow her fancy to play. Biographies are too often described as 'labours of love', but the *Roger Fry* really is in this class; one artist is writing with affection of another, so that he may be remembered and may be justified.

Finally, there are the feminist books – *A Room of One's Own* and *Three Guineas* – and several short essays, etc., some of them significant. It is as a novelist that she will be judged. But the rest of her work must be remembered, partly on its merits, partly because (as William Plomer has pointed out) she is sometimes more of a novelist in it than in her novels.

After this survey, we can state her problem. Like most novelists worth reading, she strays from the fictional norm. She dreams, designs, jokes, invokes, observes details, but she does not tell a story or weave a plot and – can she create character? That is her problem's centre. That is the point where she felt herself open to criticism – to the criticisms, for instance, of her friend Hugh Walpole. Plot and story could be set aside in favour of some other unity, but if one is writing about human beings, one does want them to seem alive. Did she get her people to live?

Now there seem to be two sorts of life in fiction, life on the page, and life eternal. Life on the page she could give; her characters never seem unreal, however slight or fantastic their lineaments, and they can be trusted to behave appropriately. Life eternal she could seldom give; she could seldom so portray a character that it was remembered afterwards on its own account, as Emma is remembered, for instance, or Dorothea Casaubon, or Sophia and Constance in *The Old Wives' Tale*. What wraiths, apart from their context, are the wind-sextet from *The Waves*, or Jacob away from *Jacob's Room*! They speak no more to us or to one another as soon as the page is turned. And this is her great difficulty. Holding on with one hand to poetry, she stretches and stretches to grasp things which are best gained by letting go of poetry. She would not let go, and I think she was quite right, though critics who like a novel to be a novel will disagree. She was quite right to cling to her specific gift, even if this entailed sacrificing something else vital to her art. And she did not always have to sacrifice; Mr and Mrs Ramsay do remain with the reader afterwards, and so perhaps do Rachel from *The Voyage Out*, and Clarissa Dalloway. For the rest – it is impossible to maintain that here is an immortal portrait gallery. Socially she is limited to the upper-middle professional classes, and she does not even employ many types. There is the bleakly honest intellectual (St John Hirst, Charles Tansley, Louis, William Dodge), the monumental majestic hero (Jacob, Percival), the pompous amorous pillar of society (Richard Dalloway as he appears in *The Voyage Out*, Hugh Whitbread), the scholar who cares only for young men (Bonamy, Neville), the pernickety independent (Mr Pepper, Mr Banks); even the Ramsays are tried out first as the Ambroses. As soon as we understand the nature of her equipment, we shall see that as regards human beings she did as well as she could. Belonging to the world of poetry, but fascinated by another world, she is always stretching out from her enchanted tree and snatching bits from the flux of daily life as they float past, and out of these bits she builds novels. She would not plunge. And she should not have plunged. She might have stayed folded up in her tree singing little songs like 'Blue-Green' in the *Monday or Tuesday* volume, but fortunately for English literature she did not do this either.

So that is her problem. She is a poet, who wants to write something as near to a novel as possible.

I must pass on to say a little – it ought to be much –

about her interests. I have emphasized her fondness for writing both seriously and in fun, and have tried to indicate how she wrote: how she gathered up her material and digested it without damaging its freshness, how she rearranged it to form unities, how she was a poet who wanted to write novels, how these novels bear upon them the marks of their strange gestation – some might say the scars. What concerns me now is the material itself, her interests, her opinions. And not to be too vague I will begin with food.

It is always helpful, when reading her, to look out for the passages which describe eating. They are invariably good. They are a sharp reminder that here is a woman who is alert sensuously. She had an enlightened greediness which gentlemen themselves might envy, and which few masculine writers have expressed. There is a little too much lamp oil in Charles Meredith's wine, a little too much paper crackling on Charles Lamb's pork, and no savour whatever in any dish of Henry James's, but when Virginia Woolf mentions nice things they get right into our mouths, so far as the edibility of print permits. We taste their deliciousness: the great dish of *Boeuf en Daube* which forms the centre of the dinner of union in *To the Lighthouse*, the dinner round which all that section of the book coheres, the dinner which exhales affection and poetry and loveliness, so that all the characters see the best in one another at last and for a moment, and one of them, Lily Briscoe, carries away a recollection of reality. Such a dinner cannot be built on a statement beneath a dish-cover which the novelist is too indifferent or incompetent to remove. Real food is necessary, and this, in fiction as in her home, she knew how to provide. The *Boeuf en Daube*, which had taken the cook three days to make and had worried Mrs Ramsay as she did her hair, stands before us, 'with its confusion of savoury brown and yellow meats and its bay leaves and its wine'; we peer down the shiny walls of the great casserole and get one of the best bits, and like William Banks, generally so hard to please, we are satisfied. Food with her was not a literary device put in to make the book seem real. She put it in because she tasted it, because she saw pictures, because she smelt flowers, because she heard Bach, because her senses were both exquisite and catholic, and were always bringing her first-hand news of the outside world. Our debt to her is in part this: she reminds us of the importance of sensation in an age which practises brutality and recommends ideals. I could have illustrated sensation more reputably by quoting the charming passage about the florist's shop in *Mrs Dalloway*, or the passage when Rachel plays upon the cabin piano. Flowers and music are conventional literary adjuncts. A good feed isn't, and that is why I preferred it and chose it to represent her reactions. Let me add that she smokes, and now let the *Boeuf en Daube* be carried away. It will never come back in our lifetime. It is not for us. But the power to appreciate it remains, and the power to appreciate all distinction.

After the senses, the intellect. She respected knowledge, she believed in wisdom. Though she could not be called an optimist, she had, very profoundly, the conviction that mind is in action against matter, and is winning new footholds in the void. That anything would be accomplished by her or in her generation, she did not suppose, but the noble blood from which she sprang encouraged her to hope.

She belonged to an age which distinguished sharply between the impermanency of man and the durability of his monuments, and for whom the dome of the British Museum Reading Room was almost eternal. Decay she admitted: the delicate grey churches in the Strand would not stand for ever; but she supposed, as we all did, that decay would be gradual. The younger generation – the Auden–Isherwood generation as it is convenient to call it – saw more clearly here than could she, and she did not quite do justice to its vision, any more than she did justice to its experiments in technique – she who had been in her time such an experimenter. Still, to belong to one's period is a common failing, and she made the most of hers. She respected and acquired knowledge, she believed in wisdom. Intellectually, no one can do more; and since she was a poet, not a philosopher or a historian or a prophetess, she had not to consider whether wisdom will prevail and whether the square upon the oblong, which Rhoda built out of the music of Mozart, will ever stand firm upon this distracted earth. The square upon the oblong. Order. Justice. Truth. She cared for these abstractions, and tried to express them through symbols, as an artist must, though she realized the inadequacy of symbols.

The next of her interests which has to be considered is society. She was not confined to sensations and intellectualism. She was a social creature, with an outlook both warm and shrewd. But it was a peculiar outlook, and we can best get at it by looking at a very peculiar side of her: her feminism.

Feminism inspired one of the most brilliant of her books – the charming and persuasive *A Room of One's Own*; it contains the Oxbridge lunch and the Fernham dinner, also the immortal encounter with the beadle when she tried to walk on the college grass, and the touching reconstruction of Shakespeare's sister – Shakespeare's equal in genius, but she perished because she had no position or money, and that has been the fate of women through the ages. But feminism is also responsible for the worst of her books – the cantankerous *Three Guineas* – and for the less successful streaks in *Orlando*. There are spots of it all over her work, and it was constantly in her mind. She was convinced that society is man-made, that the chief occupations of men are the shedding of blood, the making of money, the giving of orders, and the wearing of uniforms, and that none of these occupations is admirable. Women dress up for fun or prettiness, men for pomposity, and she had no mercy on the judge in his wig, the general in his bits and bobs of ribbon, the bishop in his robes, or even the harmless don in his gown. She felt that all these mummers were putting something across over which women had never been consulted, and which she at any rate disliked. She declined to co-operate, in theory, and sometimes in fact. She refused to sit on committees or to sign appeals, on the ground that women must not condone this tragic male-made mess, or accept the crumbs of power which men throw them occasionally from their hideous feast. Like Lysistrata, she withdrew.

In my judgement there is something old-fashioned about this extreme feminism; it dates back to her suffragette youth of the 1910s, when men kissed girls to distract them from wanting the vote, and very properly provoked her wrath. By the 1930s she had much less to complain of, and seems to keep on grumbling from habit. She complained, and rightly, that though women today have won admission into the professions and trades they usually encounter a male conspiracy when they try to get to the top. But she did not appreciate that the conspiracy is weakening yearly, and that before long women will be quite as powerful for good or evil as men. She was sensible about the past; about the present she was sometimes unreasonable. However, I speak as a man here, and as an elderly one. The best judges of her feminism are neither elderly men nor even elderly women, but young women. If they, if the students of Fernham, think that it expresses an existent grievance, they are right.

She felt herself to be not only a woman but a lady, and this gives a further twist to her social outlook. She made no bones about it. She was a lady by birth and upbringing, and it was no use being cowardly about it, and pretending that her mother had turned a mangle, or that her father Sir Leslie had been a plasterer's mate. Working-class writers often mentioned their origins, and were respected for doing so. Very well; she would mention hers. And her snobbery – for she was a snob – has more courage in it than arrogance. It is connected with her insatiable honesty, and is not, like the snobbery of Clarissa Dalloway, bland and frilled and unconsciously sinking into the best armchair. It is more like the snobbery of Kitty when she goes to tea with the Robsons; it stands up like a target for anyone to aim at who wants to. In her introduction to *Life as We Have Known It* (a collection of biographies of working-class women edited by Margaret Llewelyn Davies) she faces the fire. 'One could not be Mrs Giles of Durham, because one's body had never stood at the washtub; one's hands had never wrung and scrubbed and chopped up whatever the meat is that makes a miner's supper.' This is not disarming, and it is not intended to disarm. And if one said to her that she could after all find out what meat a miner does have for his supper if she took a little trouble, she would retort that this wouldn't help her to chop it up, and that it is not by knowing things but by doing things that one enters into the lives of people who do things. And she was not going to chop up meat. She would chop it badly, and waste her time. She was not going to wring and scrub when what she liked doing and could do was write. To murmurs of 'Lucky lady you!' she replied, 'I am a lady', and went on writing. 'There aren't going to be no more ladies. 'Ear that?' She heard. Without rancour or surprise or alarm, she heard, and drove her pen the faster. For if, as seems probable, these particular creatures are to be extinguished, how important that the last of them should get down her impressions of the world and unify them into a book! If she didn't, no one else would. Mrs Giles of Durham wouldn't. Mrs Giles would write differently, and might write better, but she could not produce *The Waves*, or a life of Roger Fry.

There is an admirable hardness here, so far as hardness can be admirable. There is not much sympathy, and I do not think she was sympathetic. She could be charming to individuals, working-class and otherwise, but it was her curiosity and her honesty that motivated her. And we must remember that sympathy, for her, entailed a tremendous and exhausting process, not lightly to be entered on. It was not a half-crown or a kind word or a good deed or a philanthropic sermon or a godlike gesture; it was adding the sorrows of another to one's own. Half fancifully, but wholly seriously, she writes:

But sympathy we cannot have. Wisest Fate says no. If her children, weighted as they already are with sorrow, were to take on them that burden too, adding in imagination other pains to their own, buildings would cease to rise; roads would peter out into grassy tracks; there would be an end of music and of painting; one great sigh alone would rise to Heaven, and the only attitudes for men and women would be those of horror and despair.

Here perhaps is the reason why she cannot be warmer and more human about Mrs Giles of Durham.

This detachment from the working classes and Labour

reinforces the detachment caused by her feminism, and her attitude to society was in consequence aloof and angular. She was fascinated, she was unafraid, but she detested mateyness, and she would make no concessions to popular journalism, and the 'let's all be friendly together' stunt. To the crowd – so far as such an entity exists – she was very jolly, but she handed out no bouquets to the middlemen who have arrogated to themselves the right of interpreting the crowd, and get paid for doing so in the daily press and on the radio. These middlemen form after all a very small clique – larger than the Bloomsbury they so tirelessly denounce, but a mere drop in the ocean of humanity. And since it was a drop whose distinction was proportionate to its size, she saw no reason to conciliate it.

Like all her friends, I miss her greatly – I knew her ever since she started writing. But this is a personal matter, and I am sure that there is no case for lamentation here. Virginia Woolf got through an immense amount of work, she gave acute pleasure in new ways, she pushed the light of the English language a little further against darkness. Those are facts. The epitaph of such an artist cannot be written by the vulgar-minded or by the lugubrious. They will try, indeed they have already tried, but their words make no sense. It is wiser, it is safer, to regard her career as a triumphant one. She triumphed over what are primly called 'difficulties', and she also triumphed in the positive sense: she brought in the spoils. And sometimes it is as a row of little silver cups that I see her work gleaming. 'These trophies,' the inscription runs, 'were won by the mind from matter, its enemy and its friend.'

Leonard Woolf

*Adapted from Malcolm Muggeridge's
BBC Television conversations with
Leonard Woolf at Monks House,
Rodmell, in March 1967*

*Leonard and Virginia Woolf lived together for many
years here at Rodmell, on the edge of the South Downs. It
was a countryside they grew to love. Their marriage was a
close and intimate partnership of two intellectuals.
Founder members of what came to be called the Bloomsbury Set. She was the daughter of a distinguished man of
letters, Sir Leslie Stephen. Brought up in a highly literary
atmosphere. Leonard Woolf's background was different.
He was born in 1880 into a comfortable middle-class Jew-
ish family.*

We were really very well off until I was twelve when my
father died. He was a Q.C. and made vast sums of money.
But he spent it all on living in a too large house, with too
many children and too many servants. Then he died quite
suddenly and my mother was left with nine children and
no money coming in. We were immediately much poorer.
We transferred ourselves to a smaller house and had three
servants instead of about eight and had to be very careful
with money. But we didn't worry very much about it.

*You were a really clever boy at school, weren't you?
You found your books easy.*

Yes, I think I did from the start. I never had any difficulty with learning things. I liked working and I liked being what used to be called 'a swot', and you were always despised if you were a swot. I have always been an unredeemed intellectual and really I think that in England one is under grave suspicion if you are an intellectual.

I suppose there were plenty of other fellow intellectuals at Cambridge?

That was the marvellous thing about life at Cambridge. Instead of feeling isolated one found friends with the same tastes who didn't despise you for being intellectual. I think it happened to be a very extraordinary time at Cambridge both among the old dons and the young dons, and also for a few years among the undergraduates.

We're talking of the turn of the century, aren't we?

Yes. I went up in 1899 and was there for five years and at Trinity there was an unusual group of dons. There were three absolutely brilliant philosophers, Bertrand Russell, Whitehead and G. E. Moore. It was one of the most extraordinary things I think, showing the inconsistency of the English government – British government I should say – that although intellect is nearly always under suspicion, and particularly theoretical intellect, there you had three philosophers of the most abstruse kind and they were all made an O.M. They were all given the Order of Merit which is the highest title I believe that you can give to people who make a name in Britain.

It is interesting. Of course, the name that one reads about in all the memoirs of people of your generation is Moore. Why was this so?

Well, he is almost the only person I think I have ever

known whom one could say was a genius. He had the most extraordinary mind, tremendously analytic, and could eventually see through almost anything. He was very original in pure thought. Bertrand Russell had the quickest mind that you could possibly conceive and he used very often to come to Moore's room when he had some philosophical difficulty and discuss it with Moore. It always seemed that together they were the hare and the tortoise: Bertie was a hare and Moore was a very slow thinking tortoise, but the tortoise nearly always won in the end.

And yet I suppose Moore's name and his books are almost unknown today?

I think that *Principia Ethica*, which is reprinted now and again, is read to a certain extent. I suppose he was never very well known outside Cambridge and philosophy.

I was interested when you said he was a genius. What does that mean exactly to you, a genius? Was Virginia a genius?

Yes, I think she was, and I think Moore was too. All geniuses are obviously not the same, you can be a genius in one way and somebody else can be a genius in another. Moore had this frightfully good and imaginative mind, but he also had an extraordinary character which I think was what made an enormous impression upon people, and you felt that he had a terrific passion. He had a passion for truth such as I have never met in any other person. He had a passion for playing the piano, he had a passion for playing fives, and this went all through his life and made him quite unlike any other person that I have ever come across. He had an enormous effect upon all of us.

Was he a major influence on you?

Absolutely a major influence on me and all my generation.

What about your own particular friends, the friends you made at Cambridge, who were the special ones?

Well, in my year there was Lytton Strachey, Saxon Sydney-Turner, Thoby Stephen, and Clive Bell. We all became very great friends. Immediately after we came up Maynard Keynes joined us and became a great friend too. I think they were a rather remarkable set of people. For instance, Maynard transformed the theory of economics and government and how to deal with unemployment. Lytton revolutionized biography with *Eminent Victorians* and *Queen Victoria*.

Undoubtedly he did.

And I think the main thing about those years, 1899 to 1904, which people now forget is that there was a revolution against Victorianism which had been begun by Shaw and Wells and Hardy and by Butler's *Way of All Flesh*, and that we more or less carried it on. It was very exciting to be trying to get a new outlook upon so many different things.

They remained your friends, didn't they? I mean those were friendships which ran on through your life.

They ran on, and of course we formed what came to be called, unfortunately, Bloomsbury. All of us who had been in that circle at Cambridge found ourselves living together in Bloomsbury, so that we were in and out of one another's houses almost as if we were still in the Cambridge courts.

It was through Thoby Stephen, presumably, that you met his sisters, Virginia and Vanessa?

Yes.

How exactly did the meeting happen?

Well, Virginia and Vanessa came up one year for that extraordinary ceremony called May Week, and they stayed with their aunt, Kate Stephen, who was Principal of Newnham. They were to come to tea with their brother Thoby, but in those days sisters couldn't have tea with their brother in Great Court Trinity unless they were chaperoned, so Kate Stephen came as well. Lytton and I were asked to meet them at tea. I had never seen them before and I had never seen Kate. Virginia and Vanessa were amazingly beautiful in white dresses and quite enormous hats. They had a great effect upon anyone who saw them at that time. They were also very fierce and silent – as most young ladies were, I suppose, in 1902. Then I went to see Thoby in London at his house in Hyde Park Gate and there I met Sir Leslie Stephen, their father, who was a most remarkable character. You had to shout down an ear trumpet to make him hear and, like many very distinguished old gentlemen of the Victorian era, he groaned a great deal. He had no compunction whatsoever about groaning and saying quite loudly what he was thinking, apparently believing that nobody could hear him. He had a great friend, an old gentleman called Gibbs, who'd been the tutor to Edward the Seventh. He used to come once a week to dine with the Stephens and by about ten o'clock Sir Leslie used to groan and say, 'Oh I wish he would go, I wish he would go home', quite loudly so that everyone heard him including Mr Gibbs.

How extraordinary. Did you feel tremendously in love

with Virginia or her sister – I mean did you feel very uplifted by them?

I was rather frightened of them and at the same time extremely attracted by them. They were amazingly beautiful, there was no doubt about it.

But you didn't imagine that you were going to marry one of them?

No, I certainly didn't until I came back from Ceylon in 1912, which was ten years later.

Were you still frightened of them?

No. I think that one of the things that happens to you as you grow older is that you get less frightened, and I think that Ceylon made me less frightened of people – including young ladies.

You could face them?

I could face them quite well when I came back.

Even when they were blue-stockings?

Yes. But of course they weren't blue-stockings. It's much easier to face a blue-stocking than a very sophisticated and contemptuous young lady.

Were they contemptuous?

Yes they were, really. You felt at the back of your mind they were frightfully – well I wouldn't say contemptuous – but critical of anything which wasn't up to the standard of the Stephens.

And that was a very high standard?

It was the tremendously high intellectual standard which was in that particular section of upper-middle-class people in the nineteenth century who provided all the rulers of India and the empire and all the judges and higher civil servants, and that's what they came from.

Were the two girls snobs, would you say?

Yes, I always told Virginia that she was an intellectual snob. I think they did really agree that they were.

The Woolf marriage was not in a conventional sense romantic. A common interest in both literature and politics drew them together rather than any overwhelming passion. They lived first in London, naturally in Bloomsbury. They came to Rodmell in 1919, and it was here that Virginia wrote most of her novels.

I feel that Monks House is still very much as it was when you first came to it, Leonard?

Up to a point, but there are of course differences. We built out the attic room by adding a window and a verandah. At the other end of the house we built on two rooms, which made it much larger. But before coming here we leased Asheham House which is across the river near Lewes.

Did you know this house when you were living at Asheham?

Yes, we very often came over to the post office in Rodmell and walked down the lane by the church where we could see over the wall into Monks House. The orchard was always very beautiful.

Did you have any idea then that you might live here?

No, never. But when old Jacob Verrall died in 1919 we heard that it was going to be put up for auction so we decided to buy the house if we possibly could. We bid at the auction and got it.

Had Jacob Verrall lived in it for some time?

Verrall acquired it I think in the seventies. He was a very strange old man. He used to lie in bed with a rope attached to his toe and at the other end of the rope there was a bell placed in a cherry tree down the garden. When the birds came to eat the cherries he gave his toe a jerk, rang the bell and scared the birds away. It was typical of Rodmell village, I should think, in those days.

That is a marvellous story. But I suppose there must be some sombre side to your memories of this house through Virginia's breakdowns when you first came here. When did they begin?

Well really of course long before we bought this house. When we married in 1912 I didn't know at all that she was liable to have these mental breakdowns. She had had one breakdown before we married when she was considerably younger, after her mother died, the strain of it brought on a mental breakdown and she tried to commit suicide then by jumping out of a window. Then after we married she got into a nervous state, she was finishing *The Voyage Out*, her first novel, and the strain of finishing a novel always brought on the symptoms.

What were they?

Any strain, any fatigue, either mental or physical, I mean whether she went on too long a walk, or stayed up too late and went to parties or overworked, would bring on these symptoms, and the first symptom was a headache and a peculiar pain at the back of the neck, which I think is universal in that form of what was called neurasthenia in those days. Then her thoughts would begin to race through her mind and she couldn't sleep. She was always a bad sleeper. And if that was allowed to go on she reached the state in which she couldn't think of anything clearly, and it became worse and worse until she was eventually what everyone would call insane.

Virginia was a creature of extremes. Either up in the skies or sunk in depression. When the latter mood took full possession of her she was mad. Leonard Woolf at such times looked after her patiently and devotedly. In 1941, borne down by despair, she committed suicide. It was a tragic end to a life which nonetheless had known long periods of happiness.

You see, she was very often referred to as if she were an invalid lady living in a drawing room and never going out, but it was entirely untrue. She was a most adventurous person. She went on the Dreadnought hoax as an Abyssinian Prince and had the most exciting time hoaxing the navy, and she lived an ordinary happy life amongst her friends.

You had a tremendous number of friends?

We had a great many, based largely on the original Cambridge circle who of course became Virginia's too.

You're in an extraordinary situation in a way, aren't you? The survivor of this group of absolutely brilliant people who dominated the intellectual life of England, internationally known. How do you feel about their achievements as a whole? How well have they worn?

It is very difficult to say. I suppose Maynard Keynes is the most certain to have left a permanent mark because he altered the whole attitude to economics and to a great extent government, and that lasts of course.

Sometimes one had the feeling that they were the fag-end of a civilization. Perhaps that isn't quite what I mean – they were so finely spun that there may be something a little thin about what they did.

Yes. It's very difficult for me to feel that altogether, but I see what you mean. I don't think it's true of Maynard who was a very practical man in enormously different ways. And Roger Fry for instance, he wasn't thin exactly, and I don't think that could be said about Vanessa and Duncan Grant, nor about Virginia's work.

Yes, I can see that. Perhaps thin is the wrong word – over – almost over-civilized.

Well, yes. There's Tom Eliot of course, one feels that about his work. It's the most extraordinary intellectual poetry and doesn't exactly have its roots in ordinary life.

That's perhaps the point. Didn't they in a way exclude a lot of ordinary life from their vision?

Some of them did – Tom of course was always trying to get back to ordinary life. I don't think he succeeded. I don't think Virginia really excluded anything from ordinary life. It was a background of that Cambridge generation which was so extraordinarily specialized in intellect that gives that impression.

Considering Leonard Woolf's friends and interests at Cambridge, it was surprising in a way that he chose to go into the Ceylon Civil Service. And yet in many respects the life suited him. He liked the remoteness, the responsibility, even the loneliness, which induced in him a lifelong love for the company of animals.

As soon as I arrived in Ceylon I was put in charge of a province without any experience whatsoever.

Did you like the authority and the power?

In a way I liked it, but as it increased I began to realize that it was a very bad thing for my character and for their character.

In other words, you felt in the end that the British rule was wrong?

Yes, gradually. When I first went out I didn't think that at all. I was unpolitical really.

Virginia wouldn't have been a very appropriate wife for a colonial administrator?

She would have been hopeless. For one thing the climate would have killed her. It would have been absolutely impossible.

I suppose your colonial experience really led you into politics. At what point did you consciously become a Socialist?

Immediately after I returned from Ceylon. I didn't know very much about English politics but the moment I became immersed in it I became a Socialist and joined the Fabian Society.

Of course, politics thenceforth played a big part in your life?

A big part through the Fabian Society, but then still more through the Labour Party.

Then of course you were tremendously interested in international affairs like the starting of the League of Nations.

I became deeply involved in that during the First World War. I was asked by the Fabian Society to deal with the possibility of preventing war, and wrote *International Government*. Sidney Webb and I really drafted on that the first treaty which would establish the League of Nations. And then we founded the League of Nations Society which went on to the League of Nations Union. And that began the whole propaganda for a League and finally the establishment.

Considering the state of the world today one wonders if all the effort you have put into the parties – the Fabian Society, the Labour Party, promotion of the League of Nations and then the United Nations – has in the end been worthwhile. I mean for someone like you who has been so dedicated a worker in all this.

I don't quite know what worthwhile means. I suppose it was worthwhile doing it, but the result seems almost negligible. The War destroyed practically all international hope of preventing war.

But still – if you had your time again?

I would do exactly the same.

Do you mind being old, Leonard?

No, I don't really mind very much. Sometimes I have a qualm, but no, I don't mind very much. I take it philosophically. You can't do anything about it.

That's absolutely true. What about the prospect of dying?

Well, that is a very hard thing, I think. I strongly object to it that one should be snuffed out, and I think one is completely snuffed out.

You have no feeling whatever of anything happening?

No, I find it impossible to believe that one would have any kind of future. It seems to me that when the body goes, the mind goes.

You think then that Virginia has gone for ever?

For ever, I think, yes. I have no belief whatsoever. In fact I have a strong disbelief. If there was a God I would be very angry with him for snuffing me out and arranging the whole thing so hopelessly badly.

I must say it is a pleasing picture to me of the Gates of Heaven opening, and you going furiously in to make your protest.

Well, I like to think that if I ever find myself in that position the first thing I should do, as I said in my book, would be to ask the Almighty whether I was right in a certain decision that I gave in court in Ceylon. The supreme court upset my judgement and I am still convinced that I was right. My second would be the protest.

Leonard, in this beautiful garden I find it impossible not to keep thinking of Virginia.

Well, I feel that she's almost an integral part of it because she was so fond of it.

And worked in it?

Yes, worked in it.

How do you think her books will stand in posterity's eyes?

It is impossible really for a contemporary to know that. But personally the only one I feel certain of being a work of genius is *The Waves*. Possibly also *Between the Acts* and possibly *To the Lighthouse*.

I have a copy here of T. S. Eliot's The Waste Land *which you and Virginia printed and published. I think it is the very first one.*

Yes, that's the first edition.

Did it take you a long time to get into the way of printing?

Quite a time, yes. Our first book was terribly badly printed. We didn't know that you had to register the plate on the back of a page with the one on the front, and so the lines were not even.

Leonard Woolf started the Hogarth Press with the thought that type-setting might provide therapy to ease Virginia's mental stress. From the beginning he saw that his marriage to this brilliant novelist involved helping and supporting her in her fight against insanity. As it turned out, a losing fight which ended in her suicide in 1941. I know of no more touching scene in literary history than that of the Woolfs pedalling their old-fashioned hand-press to print off the first copies of Eliot's Waste Land *which Virginia had set. In the event, the Hogarth Press proved a great success.*

I think you must be almost the only person who has succeeded with a one-man publishing venture?

Well, I don't know about the only person, but of course we had the great advantage that we didn't mean to be publishers.

It just happened?

It was pure chance really. We thought it would be amusing to learn to print and I thought it would be good for Virginia to have something to do manually. We tried to be taught by professionals at the St Bride's School of Printing, but we weren't allowed to because we would have had to be apprentices in order to go there.

So you had to learn yourselves?

We simply got a little pamphlet and some type and a small machine from Farringdon Road in London and learnt it.

Of course I suppose it was an enormous advantage that you had no overheads – or minimal overheads.

I think it was under fifty pounds for ten years, our actual capital investment in the place, and no overheads at all because we hadn't got any staff and we did all the work in the drawing-room.

I must say I saw your list, and without flattering you I don't think there was another publisher in London at that time who had a better list.

The authors were mostly unknown then, but subsequently they became famous.

Now you had Eliot, Virginia of course, Vita Sackville-West, Katherine Mansfield.

We published almost the first thing that Katherine Mansfield wrote, though I think she had published one book before coming to us.

Looking back to the writers that you published or knew – though of course Virginia was someone very special – which one do you now rate highest?

Well, I think T. S. Eliot. His *Waste Land*, which we were the first to publish, had more effect on poetry than any other poetic work since Coleridge and Wordsworth.

Since the Lyrical Ballads.

Yes. They created a new style of poetry, and Tom's *Waste Land* did the same.

Of course, he became a personal friend.

He was really a personal friend before we published the book. He was a strange character. When we first knew him he was extraordinarily respectable and buttoned up and inhibited, but we liked him very much. Obviously he was a genius, I think, of a sort. And then we asked him to come down here and he came and was extremely nice. Eventually he became much less inhibited and we became great friends and could talk about almost anything in the end.

How many copies of The Waste Land *did you print?*

We printed about a hundred and fifty copies of it.

Did they sell?

They sold out, slowly. Of course it was several years before he became at all well known. Nobody would publish his poems in book form at that time. His early poems were laughed at quite a lot and were thought to be absurd and unintelligible.

Did Virginia have any of her rather delightful tart remarks to make about him in her diary?

There are about everyone, including Tom. But she was very fond of him and he was very fond of her.

But in her diary she made some amusing remarks?

She generally managed to deflate people. I think quite rightly.

So do I. You don't expect me to disagree with that.

No, I don't.

But it's an important thing this journal, Leonard. Are there many volumes to it?

There's a volume for every year from 1915 to 1941.

And only a little bit of it published?

A very small part. I only published the things about her writing.

I suppose it will all be published sometime.

Well yes, but years after I am dead I should think. It couldn't be published as long as people are alive who are mentioned in it.

Because it's a bit sharp at times?

Very sharp, yes.

What was your impression of other writers in those early days, the ones you did not publish – H. G. Wells for instance?

He was a very erratic writer, but he wrote one very good book, his *History of the World*. And he produced a great many new ideas through his books.

Were you interested in Henry James?

He had an enormous influence on us when we were at

Cambridge and we became absolutely obsessed with him. We talked Henry James, wrote Henry James.

And now?

Now I think he was a very good writer, but I feel that we overestimated him. He was not a really great writer.

Did you know him?

Yes we did. He was a very strange man. I remember Virginia telling me of an amusing incident that happened when she and her brothers were children. He was great friends with Leslie Stephen and used to come and have tea with the Stephen family. He would talk as he always did – in enormous sentences, and at the same time tilt his chair back while holding on to the table. The children always hoped he would fall over backwards. And one day he did.

How marvellous.

The whole Stephen family was delighted. However, he went on finishing his sentence on the floor.

What did he think about Virginia's novels?

I don't know but I imagine that he would not have been able to stand them. He was frightfully critical of the younger generation, but he thought that Hugh Walpole was the best.

It's a curious judgement isn't it, absolutely extraordinary, because Walpole really is a forgotten man and I think rightly, don't you?

Yes, I think so. But his first book *The Schoolmaster* was rather good.

I always feel, you know, that Maugham really killed

him with Cakes and Ale. *It's a terrible thing but if you produce a first-rate satirical account of someone, unless they're very good, it does kill them.*

And it very nearly killed him personally.

Yes, I'm sure.

He was absolutely devastated by it.

Yes, I can imagine.

He came to see us and told us the whole story of how he took the book up to bed and sat on his bed undressing and had one sock off when he suddenly realized that it was about him, and he sat and read it – read it right through – and never took the other sock off. He stayed with us till three in the morning bewailing. He really was in an appalling state. It was a cruel thing.

It was cruel. But I'm afraid I enjoyed it, Leonard.

Yes, so did I to a certain extent.

What about James Joyce? I saw in your study that you had the first edition of Ulysses – *the Paris edition.*

Joyce's *Ulysses* in manuscript was submitted to us for the Hogarth Press. Tom Eliot had seen part of it and asked us whether we would consider it. We read it in manuscript and decided that we would publish it if we could find a printer to print it, but we couldn't find one who would take the risk. We had to send it back. Then it was taken to Paris and published in France by Shakespeare & Company.

It would have been a terrific thing if you had published Ulysses *and* The Waste Land. *Did you know Joyce?*

No. We never met him at all.

One of the things about the Hogarth Press that is so interesting is the way you kept careful accounts of its earnings and also your and Virginia's earnings. I was astonished to see how little she earned.

It is really rather amazing – of course Virginia never published a novel until she was thirty-five, which is late. *The Voyage Out* and *Night and Day*, I think, both took ten years to sell two thousand copies. So she was forty-five before she earned by her books more than about fifty or sixty pounds a year.

Even from her reviewing and writing, as I recall, she had microscopic earnings.

Absolutely minute. If she had to earn her living I don't think she would ever have written a novel.

It is a terrible thought. I wonder if it would be so today.

Probably, I think. It takes a very long time for that sort of writer to get across. You see she had to write five books before she had any kind of real success.

Virginia wrote with great intensity and effort, reaching a kind of ecstasy of inspiration and then correspondingly falling into the pit of despair. As we know from her journal, the strain of her writing taxed her precarious mental equilibrium, while stopping writing was liable to bring on bouts of depression. It was an appalling dilemma whose fluctuations in all their poignancy can be read as she recorded them day by day in her journal.

(reading diary) This is an interesting piece because it's what she wrote about finishing *The Waves*.

'Here in the few minutes that remain, I must record, heaven be praised, the end of *The Waves*. I wrote the words "O Death" fifteen minutes ago, having reeled across the last ten pages with some moments of such intensity and intoxication that I seemed only to stumble after my own voice; after some sort of speaker as when I was mad.'

Virginia's intermittent bouts of madness were the converse side of her genius – the sombre background against which her sparkle, her subtlety, her originality, her gaiety, her delight in people and companionship shone the more brightly.

For you, Leonard, the alternations must have been an appalling strain: sitting over meals for hours, coaxing her to eat, dreading a step in the night, hiding away the means of self-destruction.

She had alternations of what are called manic depression now. She could be very excited and exhilarated in a completely irrational way, talking in this state for days, until she became completely incoherent. I mean, the words meant nothing. Then she would fall into a coma, lasting for two days; and finally come to, and gradually recover.

It must have been absolutely hellish for you. But I have always been tremendously interested in the connection between her mental collapse and her writing. There must have been, of course, a connection.

I think it really is that her sort of genius was connected with her sort of madness and that you could see it in the way that her mind worked when she was perfectly sane. First of all in her own conversation she would do what I called 'leave the ground'. Suddenly she would begin telling one something quite ordinary, an incident she'd seen in the street or something like that; and when her mind seemed to get completely off the ground she would give the most fascinating and amusing description of something fantastic, quite unlike anything that anyone other than herself would have thought of, which would last for about five or ten minutes.

Of course that is what is meant by inspiration. We have all felt it to a minute degree – that one is racing after some meaning that is ahead of us.

Yes. And not only that, I think that very rarely, when one is writing, suddenly a thought or phrase comes into one's mind which seems to be out of one's control; that one hadn't thought of it oneself. And I think that, with people who are inclined to be mad and also inclined to be geniuses, that goes on with much greater intensity.

Blake was an example.

Yes.

I mean he barely understood himself. But then, Leonard, how did it happen that this ecstasy was combined with this black despair, and led her in the end to take her own life?

I think it was an exaggeration of what everyone feels. You get out of bed one day on the wrong side and you're miserable, and the next day you get out of bed in the morning, and you're exhilarated. And if you're exhilarated, it's ten to one that you will be depressed before the evening. My nurse always used to say that there'll be tears before the evening, if I was very excited. You see, I think that the exhilaration of her inspiration, of her writing, was followed by a depression. Both were not really under her control and much more violent than ordinary people's. Her depression would become so great that she would think life was no longer worth living.

And end it.

And end it.

What do you feel about suicide?

I think it's a lamentable thing as it happens, but I think if life isn't worth living one ought to commit suicide. I can't feel that I would, but I've got no objection to other people doing it if they want to.

You don't feel that society should set its face against it?

No.

Which of course has been the Christian attitude, hasn't it? You don't approve of that?

No, I think it's absurd. Don't you?

Well, I don't actually, no, because I think that you've got to – that society must discourage people from doing this.

Yes, but it's absurd. If you commit suicide, you're done for, you can't be punished. You're only punished for not succeeding in committing suicide.

I agree that it's illogical, but it still remains clear to me that it is absolutely terrible that such a thing should happen.

Oh, it's appalling – and also the process. If one had

seen it, as I did, seen it with one's own eyes. It's only if there has been an unbearable amount of mental torture such as she went through when she felt that she was going mad and that she couldn't control her thoughts, it was only when she got to that stage that she committed suicide, and of course the process of getting to that stage was absolutely appalling to watch.

Agony, I should think. But you must have been aware all the time that this was liable to happen.

Oh yes. As soon as I realized what it was, of course, it was what one had to guard against. Not that at any moment she would have committed suicide, because that wasn't the case. The process by which anyone with that mental disease, because it really is a disease, reaches the suicide stage is quite a long process. At times she would be perfectly all right and walk out into the garden without any danger of committing suicide. It was only after one of these long attacks in which she got more and more depressed and couldn't sleep or write, or work or see people, then she felt that she would never recover and would try to commit suicide.

Was it the price she paid for producing her books?

Yes, I think it was really.

Notes on Contributors

BARBARA BAGENAL: Born in 1891. Studied drawing and painting in Paris, and at the Slade School, London. Was a close friend of Carrington's at the Slade and soon got to know Vanessa Bell, Saxon Sydney-Turner, Lytton Strachey, Maynard Keynes, and other members of the original Bloomsbury Group – meeting at Lady Ottoline Morrell's 'Thursday Evenings'. In 1917, helped Leonard and Virginia Woolf to print Katherine Mansfield's *Prelude*. Married Nicholas Bagenal in 1918: one daughter, two sons. Now lives in Sussex.

CLIVE BELL: Writer on art and literature, and one of the original members of the Bloomsbury Group. Born in Wiltshire in 1881. Educated at Marlborough and at Trinity College, Cambridge, where he was a contemporary of Leonard Woolf. Married Vanessa Stephen, painter, sister of Virginia Woolf, in 1907. Chevalier de la Légion d'honneur, 1936. Lived at 46 Gordon Square, London; and at Charleston, Firle, Sussex. Died at Charleston in 1964.

ELIZABETH BOWEN: C.B.E., T.C.D., Hon. D.Litt. (Oxon.). Writer of fiction, literary criticism, biography, history. Born in Dublin. Lived at Bowen's Court, Kildorrery, Co. Cork. Spent her childhood between Kildorrery and Dublin. Educated at Downe House, Downe, Kent. Married, in 1923, Alan Charles Cameron (deceased). Travelled extensively, particularly in Italy and America. Lived in Hythe, Kent; and Chelsea, London. Died 1973.

LORD DAVID CECIL: C.H., M.A. (Oxon.), Hon. D.Litt. (Leeds & London), Hon. LL.D. (St Andrews & Liverpool). Writer of biography and literary criticism. Born in London in 1902. Younger son of 4th Marquess of Salisbury. Educated at Eton and at Christ Church, Oxford. In 1932 married Rachel, daughter of the late Sir Desmond MacCarthy: two sons, one daughter. Fellow New College, Oxford, 1939–69. Goldsmith Professor of English Literature, Oxford, 1948–70. Lives in Cranborne, Dorset.

ANGUS DAVIDSON: Born in 1898. Educated at Harrow and at Magdalene College, Cambridge. Served in the First World War with the Highland Light Infantry; and in the Second, with the Italian Section of the BBC European Service. Literary reviewer, art critic, translator of many books from the Italian. Authority on Edward Lear as writer and painter; author of the biography, *Edward Lear* (1938). Lives in Brighton, Sussex.

THOMAS STEARNS ELIOT: O.M., A.M. (Harvard), Hon. D.Litt. (Oxon.) and other universities; Nobel Prize for Literature, 1948. Poet, playright and publisher, his best-known works include: *The Waste Land* (1922), *Murder in the Cathedral* (1935), *Four Quartets* (1943). Born in 1888 in St Louis, Missouri. Educated at Harvard, the Sorbonne and at Merton College, Oxford. Master at Highgate Junior School, 1916. Worked for short time at Lloyd's Bank, Cornhill, London. Director of Faber & Faber, 1925–65. Became British subject, 1927. Married Valerie Fletcher, 1957. (His first wife, whom he married in 1917, died in 1947.) Died in 1965; buried at East Coker, Somerset.

EDWARD MORGAN FORSTER: C.H., Hon. Fellowship King's College, Cambridge, 1946, Hon. D.Litt. (Liverpool) and other universities. Writer of biography and literary criticism and author of five novels, including *Howards End* (1910), *A Passage to India* (1924). Joint librettist (with Eric Crozier) for Benjamin Britten's opera *Billy Budd*. Born in

London, 1879. Educated at Tonbridge School and at King's College, Cambridge. Had a lifelong connection with King's. Died in Cambridge in 1970.

MADGE GARLAND: Hon. A.R.C.A. Born in Melbourne, Australia. Educated at a private school in Paris, and then at Bedford College, London. Married (1st) Ewart Garland; (2nd) Sir Leigh Ashton in 1952. Fashion Editor of *Vogue* magazine from mid-twenties to 1940. Founded the School of Fashion, Royal College of Art, in 1950. Author of *The Changing Face of Beauty*, *The Changing Face of Childhood*, *Fashion*, *The Indecisive Decade*, *The Changing Form of Fashion*. Lives in London.

ANGELICA GARNETT: Painter. Born at Charleston, Firle, Sussex, in 1918. Niece of Virginia Woolf (and daughter of Vanessa Bell). Educated at Langford Grove School and at Maldon, Essex. Studied painting and drawing at the Euston Road School, London. Married David Garnett in 1942: four daughters. Likes travelling abroad and 'plays the piano and violin badly but with immense enjoyment'. Lives in London.

DAVID GARNETT: C.B.E., a Fellow of the Imperial College of Science and Technology (where he spent five years training as a biologist and doing research, but later abandoned science for literature). Has written many novels and edited the *Letters of T. E. Lawrence* (1938); and *Carrington: Letters and Extracts from Her Diaries* (1970). Born in Brighton in 1892. Married (1st) Rachel Marshall (d.1940): two sons; (2nd) Angelica Bell in 1942: four daughters. Lives in London and in France.

DUNCAN GRANT: Painter. Born in Scotland in 1885. Educated at St Paul's School, London, spending his holidays with his father's sister, Lady Strachey (and the large Strachey family), while his father was serving as a regular soldier in India. In 1902, he went to the Westminster School of Art. Studied art in Italy and France – and was influenced by the work of the Post-Impressionists. Returned to London and took a studio in Fitzroy Square, where he met many members of the Bloomsbury Group. Lives at Charleston, Firle, Sussex.

CHRISTOPHER ISHERWOOD: Writer of fiction, biography, and of plays in collaboration with W. H. Auden; author of many novels, including *Mr Norris Changes Trains* (1935) and *Goodbye to Berlin* (1939). Born in Cheshire, 1904. Educated at Repton School and at Corpus Christi, Cambridge. He was a medical student in London; a teacher of English in Berlin; and for a while worked for Gaumont-British and Metro-Goldwyn-Mayer. Became a citizen of the United States in 1946. Has held appointments at universities in Los Angeles and California. Now lives at Santa Monica, California.

JOHN LEHMANN: C.B.E., F.R.S.L. The young poet to whom Virginia Woolf addressed *A Letter to a Young Poet*, published 1932. Born in Buckinghamshire in 1907. Brother of Helen, Rosamond and Beatrix Lehmann. Educated at Eton and at Trinity College, Cambridge. Poet, editor, literary critic and author of many publications. Partner and General Manager of the Hogarth Press, 1938–46. Managing Director of John Lehmann Ltd, 1946–53. Founder and Editor of *New Writing, Orpheus* and the *London Magazine* (which he ceased to edit in 1961). Visiting Professor to the University of Texas at Austin and San Diego State College since 1970.

ROSAMOND LEHMANN: Born in Buckinghamshire. Sister of Helen, Beatrix and John Lehmann. Educated privately and at Girton College, Cambridge. Married the Hon. Wogan Philipps in 1928: one son, one daughter (d. 1958). Director of John Lehmann Ltd, 1946–53. Awarded Denyse Clairouin Prize for translation of Jacques Lemarchand's novel, *Geneviève*. Writer of many novels, including *Dusty Answer* (1927), *Invitation to the Waltz* (1932), *The*

Ballad and the Source (1944); and of the play, *No More Music* (1939). Lives in London.

DAME ROSE MACAULAY: D.B.E. Poet, essayist, novelist. Born in Rugby, 1881. Attended convent school, Varazze, when her parents moved to Italy; on their return to England went to High School, Oxford; and then read History at Somerville College, Oxford. After leaving college wrote first novel, *Abbots Verney* (1906). Took job in War Office in 1917. Since childhood delighted in writing poetry (2 vols. published: 1914, 1917). The best known of her many novels are *The World My Wilderness* (1950) and *The Towers of Trebizond* (1956). Died in 1958.

FRANCES MARSHALL: Translator from Spanish and French; has had over twenty titles published. Born in London, 1900. Educated at Bedales School, Hampshire, and at Newnham College, Cambridge. Assistant to Francis Birrell and David Garnett in their bookshop at Taviton Street (and then Gerrard Street), London. In 1933, married Ralph Partridge (d. 1960): one son, Lytton Burgo (1935–63). Under the editorship of Lytton Strachey, helped Ralph Partridge to edit the complete edition of the *Greville Memoirs* (1938). Lives in London.

LOUIE MAYER: Mentioned as Louie Everest (1st marriage, 1929) in Leonard Woolf's volumes of autobiography. Born in Eastdean, Sussex, in 1912. Lived at Burwash when her father worked on the Rudyard Kipling Estate, then at Southease. Moved with her family (two boys) to a cottage in Rodmell in 1934, and worked as cook-general for Leonard and Virginia Woolf (until Leonard Woolf's death in 1969). Diploma in Advanced Cooking, 1936. Married Konrad Mayer in 1962. Now lives near Seaford.

RAYMOND MORTIMER: C.B.E. Author, writer of biography, art and literary criticism. Literary Editor of the *New Statesman and Nation*, 1935–47. Born in 1895. Educated at Malvern and at Balliol College, Oxford. His publications include *Channel Packet* (1942), *Manet's Bar aux Folies-Bergère* (1944) and *Duncan Grant* (1944). Lives in London.

NIGEL NICOLSON: M.B.E., F.S.A. Second son of Sir Harold Nicolson and Vita Sackville-West. Born in 1917. Educated at Eton and at Balliol College, Oxford. Capt. Grenadier Guards, 1939–45. Married Philippa Tennyson d'Eyncourt in 1953: one son, two daughters. M.P. Bournemouth East and Christchurch, 1952–9. Author of many books, including *Lord of the Isles* (1960) and *Great Houses* (1968). Edited *Harold Nicolson: Diaries & Letters*. Has been director of a London publishing house since 1947. Lives at Sissinghurst Castle, Kent.

WILLIAM PLOMER: C.B.E., D.Litt., F.R.S.L. Novelist, poet, biographer. Born in South Africa in 1903, of English parents. Early years spent as trader and farmer in South Africa. Travelled to many countries, including Greece, Japan and Russia. Settled in Japan and was offered the Chair of English Literature in the Imperial University in 1928. Served as civilian officer at the Admiralty, 1940–45. Then became literary adviser to a London publishing house. Queen's Gold Medal for Poetry, 1963. Lived in Sussex. Died 1973.

GEORGE RYLANDS: M.A. Fellow, King's College, Cambridge. University Lecturer in English Literature (retd). Born 1902. Educated at Eton and at King's College, Cambridge. Worked at Hogarth Press, 1924–5. Chairman of Trustees and Directors of the Arts Theatre, Cambridge, since 1946. Governor of the Old Vic. Author of various publications. For thirty years directed (and took part in) productions of Shakespeare's plays for the Cambridge University Marlowe Dramatic Society; and other undertakings in Shakespearean drama, poetry and music recitals, etc. – including some for the BBC, and recordings for the British Council. Lives in King's College, Cambridge.

HON. VITA SACKVILLE-WEST: C.H., F.R.S.L., J.P. Born at Knole, Sevenoaks, in 1892. Daughter of 3rd Baron Sackville. Educated privately. Married the Hon. Harold Nicolson in 1913: two sons. Biographer, poet, novelist. Hawthornden Prize for *The Land* (1927). Authority on landscape gardening, flowers and plants. Created beautiful gardens at Knole, and Sissinghurst Castle, Kent. Died 1962.

STEPHEN SPENDER: C.B.E. Poet, critic. Born 1909. Educated at University College School and at University College, Oxford. Married Natasha Litvin, 1941: one son, one daughter. Served in the National Fire Service, 1941–4. Co-editor of *Horizon Magazine* (1939–41), and of *Encounter* (1953–67). Appointments at various American universities, 1953–69. Professor of English, University College, London University, since 1970. Lives in London.

ANN STEPHEN: M.B., B.Ch. (Cantab.). Daughter of Adrian Stephen (Virginia Woolf's younger brother). Born in London in 1916. Educated at Miss Fry's School, Buckinghamshire, at Newnham College, Cambridge, and at the Royal Free Hospital, London. Married (1st) Richard Llewelyn Davies in 1938 (divorced); (2nd) Dr Richard Synge, F.R.S. (Nobel Prize for Chemistry, 1952): three sons, four daughters. Has translated many scientific books and papers (mostly concerned with the origin of life) from the Swedish and Russian. Lives in Norfolk.

ALIX STRACHEY: Psychoanalyst and writer. Born in New York in 1892. Maiden name Sargant-Florence. Educated at Bedales School, Hampshire, and at Newnham College, Cambridge. Married, in 1920, James Strachey (d. 1967). Assisted James Strachey in his work of translating the complete psychological works of Sigmund Freud (23 volumes). Author of *The Unconscious Motives of War* (1957), and various papers connected with psychology. Lives in Buckinghamshire.

DAME JANET VAUGHAN: D.B.E., D.M., F.R.C.P. Born in 1899. Educated at North Foreland Lodge, at Somerville College, Oxford, and at University College Hospital, London. Married David Gourlay in 1930: two daughters. Assistant in Clinical Pathology, British Post-Graduate Medical School, 1934–9; and many other appointments. Principal, Somerville College, Oxford, 1945–67. Hon. Fellow Somerville College since 1967. Lives in Oxford.

DAME REBECCA WEST: D.B.E. Novelist, historian, literary critic, political writer. Her many books include *The Thinking Reed* (1936), *The Meaning of Treason* (1948) and *The Fountain Overflows* (1957). Born in 1892. Educated at George Watson's Ladies College, Edinburgh. Married, in 1930, Henry Maxwell Andrews (d. 1968). Joined staff of *Freewoman* as reviewer in 1911, and of *The Clarion* as political writer in 1912. Member of the American Academy of Arts and Sciences. Lives in London.

LEONARD WOOLF: B.A., Hon. D.Litt. (Sussex). Born 1880. Educated at St Paul's School and Trinity College, Cambridge. In the Ceylon Civil Service 1904–11. Married Virginia, 1912. Founded the Hogarth Press, 1917. Editor of the *International Review*, 1919. Literary Editor, *The Nation*, 1923–30. Author of many political books; of a novel, *The Village in the Jungle*; and five volumes of autobiography – the last one being published in the year of his death, 1969.

Bibliography

PRINCIPAL WORKS OF VIRGINIA WOOLF

The Voyage Out, 1915; Duckworth, London. Doran, New York, 1920. Harcourt Brace, New York, 1926.

The Mark on the Wall, 1917; Hogarth Press, Richmond. (Also in *Monday or Tuesday* and *A Haunted House*)

Kew Gardens, 1919; Hogarth Press, Richmond. (Also in *Monday or Tuesday* and *A Haunted House*)

Night and Day, 1919; Duckworth, London. Doran, New York, 1920.

Monday or Tuesday, 1921; Hogarth Press, Richmond. Harcourt Brace, New York, 1921.

Jacob's Room, 1922; Hogarth Press, Richmond. Harcourt Brace, New York, 1923.

Mr Bennett and Mrs Brown, 1924; Hogarth Press, London. (Also in *The Captain's Death Bed*)

The Common Reader, 1925; Hogarth Press, London. Harcourt Brace, New York, 1925.

Mrs Dalloway, 1925; Hogarth Press, London. Harcourt Brace, New York, 1925.

To the Lighthouse, 1927; Hogarth Press, London. Harcourt Brace, New York, 1927.

Orlando: A Biography, 1928; Hogarth Press, London. Crosby Gaige, New York, 1928. Harcourt Brace, New York, 1929.

A Room of One's Own, 1929; Hogarth Press, London. Fountain Press, New York, 1929. Harcourt Brace, New York, 1929.

On Being Ill, 1930; Hogarth Press, London. (Also in *The Moment*)

The Waves, 1931; Hogarth Press, London. Harcourt Brace, New York, 1931.

A Letter to a Young Poet, 1932; Hogarth Press, London. (Also in *The Death of the Moth*)

The Common Reader: Second Series, 1932; Hogarth Press, London. Harcourt Brace, New York, 1932.

Flush: A Biography, 1933; Hogarth Press, London. Harcourt Brace, New York, 1933.

Walter Sickert: A Conversation, 1934; Hogarth Press, London. (Also in *The Captain's Death Bed*)

The Years, 1937; Hogarth Press, London. Harcourt Brace, New York, 1937.

Three Guineas, 1938, Hogarth Press, London. Harcourt Brace, New York, 1938.

Reviewing, 1939; Hogarth Press, London. (Also in *The Captain's Death Bed*)

Roger Fry: A Biography, 1940; Hogarth Press, London. Harcourt Brace, New York, 1940.

Between the Acts, 1941; Hogarth Press, London. Harcourt Brace, New York, 1941.

The Death of the Moth, 1942; Hogarth Press, London. Harcourt Brace, New York, 1942.

A Haunted House, 1944; Hogarth Press, London. Harcourt Brace, New York, 1944.

The Moment, 1947; Hogarth Press, London. Harcourt Brace, New York, 1947.

The Captain's Death Bed, 1950; Hogarth Press, London. Harcourt Brace, New York, 1950.

A Writer's Diary, 1953; Hogarth Press, London. Harcourt Brace, New York, 1954.

Virginia Woolf and Lytton Strachey: Letters, 1956; Hogarth Press and Chatto & Windus, London. Harcourt Brace, New York, 1956.

BIBLIOGRAPHY

Granite and Rainbow: Essays, 1958; Hogarth Press, London. Harcourt Brace, New York, 1958.

Contemporary Writers, 1965; Hogarth Press, London.

Nurse Lugton's Golden Thimble, 1966; Hogarth Press, London. (A short story for children found in the MS. of *Mrs Dalloway*)

Collected Essays (4 vols.), 1967; Hogarth Press, London. Harcourt Brace, New York, 1967.

Mrs Dalloway's Party, 1973; Hogarth Press, London.

Index